SO YOU WANT TO BUY A WORD PROCESSOR?

All the Best
& Thanks for your help

@ JS

Michael Elan

So you want to buy a word processor?

Helen Harris and Ela Chauhan

Published by Business Books in association with Prolog Infotext

BUSINESS BOOKS

London Melbourne Sydney Auckland Johannesburg

Business Books Ltd
An imprint of the Hutchinson Publishing Group
17-21 Conway Street, London W1P 6JD

Hutchinson Group (Australia) Pty Ltd
30-32 Cremorne Street, Richmond South, Victoria 3121
PO Box 151, Broadway, New South Wales 2007

Hutchinson Group (NZ) Ltd
32-34 View Road, PO Box 40-086, Glenfield, Auckland 10

Hutchinson Group (SA) (Pty) Ltd
PO Box 337, Bergvlei 2012, South Africa

First published 1982

Set in 10 on 11 Optima by Wordsmiths
of Street, Somerset

Printed in Great Britain by the Anchor Press Ltd
and bound by Wm Brendon & Son Ltd
both of Tiptree, Essex

Designer: Roger Daniels
Cartoons: Nigel Paige
Line Drawings: Ted Hammond

British Library Cataloguing in Publication Data
Harris, Helen
    So you want to buy a word processor?
    1. Word processing equipment - Great Britain
    I. Title   II. Chauhan, Ela
    651.8   HF5548.2

ISBN 0 09 150351 5

Preface

This book has been inspired by the lessons learned and the experience gained since I was first introduced to word processing in the summer of 1978 while working for ICL. The intervening years were times of tremendous job satisfaction and reward, most of which can be directly attributed to the scope that word processing offered within my areas of responsibility.

That does not mean that those years were without periods of frustration and, at first, doubt concerning the application of word processing within my particular job environment. However, the doubts were certainly short-lived and the frustrations rapidly diminished with inreased knowledge and awareness concerning the equipment, its application and its impact on the organisation.

The rewards were far greater than had ever been anticipated and the job satisfaction that resulted was beyond all expectations.

HELEN HARRIS

Foreword

For many years advanced technology in the form of computers and telecommunications was the exclusive province of the technical elite. Today, with the availability of low cost, easy to use systems, there is an increasing need for a better understanding by management of how information technology can improve the efficiency of business. The introduction of word processors into the office is often the first step taken by many managers into the realm of information technology. A step that many may be reluctant to take because of their lack of knowledge about the benefits that can be realised, coupled with their fear of technology.

"So You Want To Buy A Word Processor?" removes many of these uncertainties. It provides a step-by-step guide into the way in which the word processor can be effectively introduced into the office. It is appropriate for this book to be published during Information Technology Year 1982, a campaign designed to increase the awareness of the benefits and opportunities offered by information technology amongst all sectors of the community.

I believe that proprietors of small businesses as well as managers in larger organisations will find this an invaluable aid to their understanding of word processing.

Kenneth R Barnes
Project Director
Information Technology Year 1982.

Contents

Acknowledgements

We are indebted to a number of dear friends, colleagues and other willing "guinea-pigs" for their patience in reading and constructively commenting on drafts to our text, and for their continued enthusiasm for our venture. They are:

David Becket, Nancy Darby, Krysia Goca, Henry Goldberg of ASL, Patricia de Haas, Allan Hart, Veronica Rock, Sara Turnbull of Kimball Bailey & Partners, Roger Whitehead of Office Futures, and a number of partners and managers in the firm of Goodman Jones.

We owe much to our Chairman John Harris for his contribution to the chapters on costs and contracts, and above all for his understanding, tolerance and continued encouragement during the months of preparation of the text.

We thank: Nigel Paige for his humour and for skilfully emphasising the human aspects of the subject, Roger Daniels for his design work and making the whole thing take shape, Ted Hammond for his line drawings and Tom Graves of Wordsmiths for his enthusiasm and assistance.

And we are most grateful to Kenneth Barnes for giving us recognition in his Information Technology campaign.

The following suppliers have been kind in providing photographs and material on which illustrations have been based:

CBM Data Software, CPT (UK), Data Recall, IBM United Kingdom, ICL, Office International, PCD Maltron, Perforag, The Power Equipment Company, Rank Xerox, Willis Computer Supplies, Wordplex United Kingdom.

Finally, a word of appreciation to Peter Eversden, John Myers, and Helen Townley, without whose training and encouragement during preceding years, this work would never have been contemplated.

About the Authors

Helen Harris is a Director and Managing Consultant of Prolog Infotext, the office automation consultancy. Her career has been closely concerned with the application of technology to the efficient handling of all types of information. Application areas include the pharmaceutical industry, market research, journalism and the computer industry. Helen Harris is a graduate of Aberdeen and City Universities where she took degrees in Chemistry and Information Science. She is a Member of the Institute of Information Scientists and a Founder Member of the Institute of Word Processing. She belongs to the Office Automation Network, an association of independent consultants dedicated to the task of helping commercial, administrative and educational organisations to become more effective.

Ela Chauhan has been involved with word processing since 1979. Since that time she has worked extensively in the areas of systems support, training and applications consultancy covering a variety of systems. Ela Chauhan is a senior consultant with Prolog Infotext and has worked with Helen Harris for a number of years. She studied Astrophysics at Queen Mary College, London and is a Member of the Institute of Word Processing.

John Harris who has made a significant contribution to the chapters on Costs and Contracts is Chairman of Prolog Infotext. He is also an independent consultant to the computing industry, serves on the board of a number of computer service companies, and is a past Chairman of the Computer Services Association's Turnkey Suppliers Division.

PROLOG INFOTEXT LIMITED
9 CHEPSTOW ROAD
LONDON W2 5BP
TELEPHONE 01 229 5069

Introduction

Dramatic changes have begun to take place in many of today's offices. They have been brought about by the application of microprocessor technology to routine activities. Word processing, viewdata, teletext, facsimile transmission (fax) and intelligent copying are becoming recognised features of much day-to-day office life. But the greatest impact will come from the ultimate convergence of these towards what is popularly referred to as "the automated office".

Yet so many have still to experience the benefits of taking their first steps in office automation. If you are one of these people and believe the time has come to move in that direction, beginning with investment in word processing equipment, then this book is for you. Alternatively, there will be some who have already experimented with word processors and now recognise the need to become better informed, before making a greater commitment within their organisation.

Objectives

We do not want you to be overwhelmed by the new technology, but to take it in your stride. We aim to cover the many issues that have to be considered, planned for, and implemented when selecting and acquiring word processing equipment. Appropriate action should then lead to:

□ better decision-making in selecting a system;

□ a smooth transition from existing methods; and ultimately

□ a successful installation, where the investment is well matched by the rewards.

Be aware that among some early users, there has been disillusionment and sometimes failure to meet the high returns expected. Often this has been due to inadequate planning and lack of awareness by those involved with, or affected by the introduction of word processing equipment. If we achieve our objectives, then not only will you become one of the enlightened and successful ones, it may lead you much sooner to your next step in office automation and the potential benefits which that may bring.

We have deliberately steered clear of listing individual suppliers' equipment. Word processing is a rapidly expanding and changing field. There are a number of sources available to provide up-to-date information that will help identify equipment with specific features. These sources are covered in an appendix. *Our* role is to provide the background knowledge needed to specify requirements, select a suitable system and successfully install equipment.

Market

Those are our objectives. Who are we aiming at? Your organisation may range from a small business with two or three staff, to a multinational or a government establishment. You may be the person responsible for the business or a major function within it, a departmental manager, or someone delegated the task of investigating the possibilities for word processing. The only prior knowledge assumed is a basic awareness of typing activities and office routine, with a minimum of prior exposure to the sorts of tasks that word processors can do.

Some readers will be considerably more informed than this, whether through prior reading, private research, or discussion with colleagues. But we believe the book's structure and presentation will help these people to skim over familiar topics and concentrate on matters new to them. Chapters and sections are clearly identified, points are itemised within the text and, where appropriate, key phrases have been highlighted. Checklists are provided.

We assume the reader is primarily interested in more efficient *document production or text processing*, with the processing of data or information (sometimes referred to as record or list processing) seen as possible enhancements. If however, data or information processing are just as important to you, then this book should be read in conjunction with other works specifically geared to covering those subjects.

What has led you this far?

Usually it is the result of seeking the solution to a problem or set of problems involving document production:

□ typists may continually have to amend existing text;

□ standard letters or internal memos may need to be personalised or documents may require numerous redrafts;

□ it could be a personnel problem involving dissatisfied or insufficient staff; or

□ for some, it may be the creation of business opportunities involving new publications or services, or the ability to maintain an image that matches that of competitors.

Whatever it is, the solution needs to make better use of the organisation's most important resource – its people. As staff costs continue to rise while the cost of electronic equipment falls, management must look increasingly to microprocessor technology to help solve their problems. With word processing the outcome should be more creative and skilled jobs as well as greater effectiveness and efficiency in document production. We define *effectiveness* as the extent to which the desired result is realised, and *efficiency* as the extent to which the result produced is done so at least cost.

What We Mean by Word Processing

The term was first coined in the 1960's. Strictly it means a system for getting thoughts into written communications, a system that involves people, equipment and procedures. What concerns us here is the application of microprocessor technology to help this transformation and to produce a typed document faster and more efficiently than with previous methods. In practice this means being able to type it, store it in some form of magnetic memory, recall it, alter it and print it as often as we like until completely satisfied with it – but without having to rekey unaltered sections. In addition, word processing provides the capability of automating many of the routine or repetitive aspects of typing.

Although the term is widely used today to describe equipment performing the activities we have just described, what is offered by suppliers varies enormously in system design and the extent of facilities offered. The range broadly covers:

□ an *electronic memory typewriter* looking much like an electric typewriter but using microprocessor technology to automate a range of routine operations such as centring, underlining and paragraph indenting;

□ a *microcomputer dedicated to text processing* and performing a wide range of tasks that help with editing, document lay-out (referred to as formatting), and manipulation of text;

□ a similar range of facilities provided as just *one of a number of applications on a micro*, mini or larger (mainframe) computer.

How did we arrive at this stage of development? Mechanical typing was first invented in the eighteenth century but it was not until the latter half of the nineteenth century that typewriters were produced on a commercial scale. The first *automatic* machines were introduced in the 1930's and used paper rolls, later paper tape as a form of memory. By the 1960's IBM (International Business Machines) had introduced the Selectric "golf-ball" typewriter allowing the typist to change the print element, the golf-ball, to provide a different typefount (character design and size). The next major breakthrough was the introduction of IBM's Magnetic Tape Selectric Typewriter MT/ST using magnetic tape to store text while simultaneously printing it on paper. Magnetic cards were then introduced as the storage medium. One card was used for each page of typing making the association between printed document and the storage medium easier for the typist to grasp.

The next milestone was the introduction of a *visual display*, somewhat like a television screen and referred to as a visual display unit, VDU, VT (video terminal), CRT (cathode ray tube), or just screen, which allowed the typist to see what was happening to the text as it was being typed, amended and stored, but before being committed to paper. As the typist could refer to the screen rather than the printed page to monitor progress, the printer could be treated as a separate unit working independently of the keyboard. The keyboard could be housed in a unit together with the screen or attached to it via a short cable.

The first screen-based word processor appeared in 1971 but market penetration was not achieved until 1976. The size of display can be as large as the equivalent of an A4 page, in other words 50 to 60 lines or more and generally referred to as a "full-page display". However, it is more often in tha region of 22 – 24 lines of text, called "partial-page display". A few additional lines are available for control information used by the system and provided to assist the typist or operator. Display width is generally 80 columns but can vary from this.

Another significant breakthrough was the introduction of *floppy discs* or diskettes (affectionately termed floppies) as the main external storage medium or memory. These look similar to 45 rpm records or a little smaller and are made of plastic coated with a magnetic film. Text can be recalled, changed and stored again much faster than with magnetic tape or cards. In addition to floppies many suppliers are now making available hard disc systems with considerably greater storage capacity. Hard discs are rigid rather than flexible and secured in their own sealed housing unit. Sometimes a number of hard discs are accommodated within the same unit (each

disc is referred to as a platter in this case).

We described discs as the prime medium for the external memory; word processors also have a limited internal storage facility or memory used by the system to hold the program logic (software) and as workspace. And finally, there is the processor providing the "nerve-centre" of the system and enabling it to carry out its various tasks.

Manufacturers are still developing electronic typewriters (with or without external memory) and such machines will continue to prove viable in certain situations involving the processing of words on paper. The size of display in these machines is generally one line of text from 15 to 30 characters long and referred to as a "thin-window" display. However, the cost of *screen-based, disc storage systems* is now such that these must form the prime consideration for anyone interested in extensive text editing and manipulation. The reasons for this are:

1. Sizeable sections of the document are visible during its creation helping ease of use, formatting and manipulation to give the desired lay-out.

2. Ease of visually relating what is being typed to the page finally printed. This ultimately leads to faster input and editing by the typist.

3. The document can be read on the screen by the typist and revised before being printed.

4. Paragraphs, sections and columns of text can visibly be moved around.

5. Generally, work can continue on another document or with some systems the same document, while printing a different piece of text takes place in the "background".

6. Complete page lay-outs can readily be set up, stored, recalled and followed for each new version of a standard document.

To qualify the earlier remark about electronic typewriters: one of the significant roles that these will increasingly fulfil is in getting the first draft of text into a magnetic memory, which can then be read and manipulated on a screen-based system with which the memory is compatible. Another major application area is for documents requiring little editing or

Six-line display – IBM System 6

Partial-page display – Toshiba EW-100

Partial-page display – Data Recall Diamond 5,
normally 80 columns by 32 rows

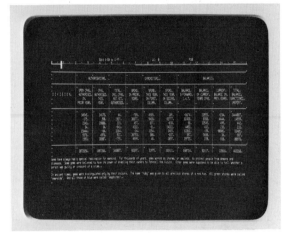

Diamond 5 screen in Wide Mode with 160 columns
by 32 rows

Full-page display – Rank Xerox 860

text manipulation but where final presentation must be of a high standard.

The range of editing facilities offered on word processors today is extensive and these are summarised in Chapter 1. We have mentioned that word processing can be just one of a vast number of applications available on a computer otherwise used for data processing activities. By the same token, systems built as dedicated word processors are being developed to provide data processing facilities through the use of additional software.

In conclusion, then, a "system" as far as this book is concerned includes a processor together with internal memory, a screen (as opposed to thin-window display), a keyboard, a printer, and a floppy or hard disc unit.

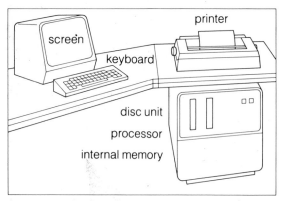

Word processing system

Structure of the Book
There are four major parts to the book. Each part has an introduction and each chapter has a checklist. Part I covers the decision to invest. Part II provides extensive coverage of what features, facilities and other criteria need to be considered in selecting equipment. If you have never seen a word processor in operation we recommend that you do so before covering Part II, in order to get the most out of it. Alternatively, you may prefer to skim the contents first, have a demonstration of equipment and then return to read the Part in more detail.

Part III looks at the people issues and matters concerning the organisation and running of a system. Part IV covers costs and contractual considerations. Then follows a brief discussion of likely developments in word processors and the convergence of equipment towards "the automated office".

There are many illustrations included and we have incorporated a number of cartoons to emphasise the need to be continually aware of the human aspects of word processing.

Three Appendices are provided. Appendix 1 gives sources of further information. Appendix 2 covers detailed considerations in the running of the system and is provided as a supplement to Chapter 10 (on responsibilities and system operation). Appendix 3 is an overall checklist for investing in word processing. To help readers then use the complete book as a reference work, a detailed index to its contents is provided.

PART I
Deciding to Invest

Part I begins by looking at the problems with which readers might currently be faced and the benefits sought in using word processing equipment. We summarise what word processors can do and discuss application areas particularly suited to word processing.

Chapter 2 provides guidance on analysing current activities, procedures, and office organisation in preparation for detailing requirements. But before covering this we look at what is involved in getting words onto paper and the different types of document produced within an office. We feel the need to caution you about the inclusion of this chapter. Many managers have only the slightest conception of what a secretary or typist's job entails and the breadth of skills these staff possess. You may have typed the odd line or two on a typewriter, but have you ever set out a table, typed with carbon copies, aligned and corrected a previously typed document, changed a printer ribbon, put together a mail-shot, used a telex machine, ...? Hence Chapter 2 must be covered, for if you do not fully understand today's problems, it will not help to automate them tomorrow.

Finally we discuss the management and organisational issues concerning the arrangement of word processing services within an establishment, the need for commitment, and project management in selecting and installing equipment. A run-down of the different types of system and of suppliers is also given.

The Application of Word Processing

Do you have you a problem?

What can a word processor do?

What type of workload benefits from word processing?

Businesses where benefits are readily identified

Checklist

Do you have a problem?

The number of word processors installed worldwide by mid-1982 was estimated to be in the region of three-quarters of a million with about five per cent of these in the UK. Ever since the first word processors were launched those in the field – suppliers, consultants, and specialists alike – have been quoting one statistic after another about rising office costs and the percentage of these that relate to labour. As labour costs rise, it is argued, so does the cost of producing paperwork. Word processing can help to check some of these rising costs.

The first convincing argument put forward is usually based on a suggestion of increased throughput of work by typing staff (number of pages typed and corrected per hour, day, week). The outcome is that staff can then be released to do other jobs, or a greater typing load can be handled. Such suggestions have been well substantiated by many users. The level of increased productivity varies tremendously depending on the type of documents processed, procedures for using the equipment, and the attitude and well-being of the staff involved. Productivity improvements of up to 400 per cent have been quoted in organisations where there is constant heavy revision of text, and several times this in those concentrating on the preparation of standard letters.

Such increases could lead to situations of redundancy, or at least to a reduction in the overall number of office jobs available. Typing staff may be freed to take on responsibilities from retiring employees or there may be less demand for agency staff to cope with peak periods. Alternatively, the creation of new jobs may be slowed down, since relevant activities can now be taken on by secretaries and typists. Others will argue that the increase can lead to more business, sufficient to justify taking on more employees. Whatever the argument, if justifications are to be based on improved productivity, the case needs to be well thought out and presented to all involved. In some organisations this will include trade unions. Those covering office workers have already examined the implications of word processing and office automation technology on their membership and have published papers on the subject.

However, organisations usually look to word processing because there is a specific problem and not as part of a deliberate strategy to reduce overall office costs. Identifying the cause may not be so easy but the symptoms are usually fairly obvious. It could be any one or a combination of the following:

- managers doing work that could be done by secretaries;

- an unhappy secretarial and typing workforce, evidenced by time spent away from the desk and a high turnover of staff, or just constant moans and groans;

- a high ratio of secretaries and typists to managers;

- frequent use of agency staff or excessive overtime being done;

- poor quality of typed output – mistakes and messy, inconsistent lay-out with little attention to house-style;

- document production deadlines not being met, or turnround from submission of work to the typed product taking too long;

- originators spending too much time proof-reading one draft after another (originators is the term we use throughout the book to refer to those generating the documents to be typed and will include managers, executives, technical writers, authors and a variety of other staff).

The overall picture is one of general dissatisfaction with document preparation services. These may involve just one typist or secretary, a group or team of such staff, or a central typing pool. The symptoms could even be more fundamental to the running of the business. As an illustration, a company may have difficulties in credit control with invoices and statements not being sent out quickly enough and follow-up letters not having sufficient impact.

Having recognised the symptoms, how can you identify the real problem(s) and decide whether word processing is the answer? Let us first look at what word processors are capable of doing and the recognised ways in which they have helped successful users.

What can a word processor do?

There are a number of basic functions or activities that all systems perform. A variety of additional and more complex features are increasingly available. However, every supplier varies in the mix of what is offered and each system will be good at doing some tasks, not so brilliant at others. The differences to be looked for in selecting equipment for your particular needs are covered in depth in Part II. But as an overview, word processors offer the following range of facilities (if some terms are unfamiliar to you, all will be revealed later).

Facilities generally included:

1. The typist does not need to worry about line endings (carriage returns), the system will automatically move a word onto the next line if it does not fit on the end of the current one. This is referred to as the "word-wrap" facility.

2. Performance of a number of other functions automatically such as centring text, sub and superscript positioning, numbering pages, putting consistent heading and footing information in the right place, pagination (splitting the text into specified page lengths), right-hand justification, and sometimes proportional spacing.

3. On revising a document, only those parts that have been altered need be (re)typed, whether as corrections, deletions or insertions. Line endings and page boundaries will be moved accordingly.

④ The ability to highlight or emphasise text by changing the typeface or by using an overstrike or emboldening (often referred to as just "bold") facility. Overstrike causes the character to be struck twice or more in exactly the same position. With bold the character is struck a number of times, each time slightly offset from the last position. The former merely blackens the character, bold gives an impression of thickness.

⑤ Documents can be recalled and the format altered at the touch of a few keys – for example, margin settings, line and character spacing, and page length.

⑥ Blocks of text can be moved around within the same document or from one document to another.

⑦ Name and address information and other personalised variables can automatically be merged into a standard piece of text such as a letter.

Additional facilities that may be offered:

① A particular word or character string can be searched for throughout a document and if necessary replaced with another.

② Columns of data or text can be moved around.

③ Lists can be sorted into alphabetic or numeric sequence.

④ The mask or overlay of a standard form can be displayed on the screen, the variable information filled in, and only the infilled data printed on the preprinted form.

⑤ A simple arithmetic capability adds and subtracts rows and columns of figures, and perhaps even multiplication, division and percentage calculations are possible.

⑥ Spelling can be checked.

In addition a word processor provides fast, good quality printing and may allow communication with similar word processors, a larger computer or other electronic equipment. Further applications which are strictly non-text editing, but which might usefully be interfaced with the word processing software, are becoming available to run on the same machines. Examples are management accounting, stock control, sales and purchase ledger, invoicing and ordering, and mathematical calculations. Evaluation of such applications must be the subject of a separate study, *any* invoicing system, just like any word processing system will not necessarily be the best solution for *you*.

What type of workload benefits from word processing?

Taking into account the primary features mentioned above, word processors consistently show most benefit when a large proportion of the work can be described as one or a combination of the following types of document.

① Standard correspondence or similar documentation that needs to be personalised.

② Documents requiring extensive revision before they are ready for the final copy – procedures, technical documentation, press releases, brochures, management reports and the like.

③ Documents that require first-class presentation. The standard required may necessitate the document normally having to be completely retyped even for minor mistakes.

④ Documents involving standard sections of text brought together in various ways for each version. Examples are specifications, proposals, leases and other legal documents.

⑤ Documents that are updated regularly with a relatively small proportion of the information being changed. Examples are directories, catalogues, inventories, financial and statistical reports.

⑥ Lists that need to be organised and maintained in a particular sequence.

⑦ Documents with publication deadlines, but which are dependent on information from a variety of sources – for example, newsletters, abstract bulletins, and departmental progress reports.

Businesses where benefits are readily identified

Most organisations are likely to be involved in at least one of those areas of document production. Whether or not to an extent which yet justifies investment in word processing is another matter. By the nature of their activities some businesses or professions lend themselves well to word processing applications because the written word is the very substance of the product or service being offered. One well-quoted example is *the legal profession*: the primary product of a lawyer's office, it has been said, is not justice but paperwork! Paperwork such as wills, leases, statements, contracts and other agreements with their very precise language require one revision after another, while also relying on standard paragraphs and phrases. *Sales and consultancy organisations* putting together lengthy proposals and tenders to win new business similarly generate many drafts and use standard sections of text.

Any organisation involved in extensive mail-shots where the personal approach is desirable is already likely to be using word processing. *Personnel functions* generate standard yet personalised correspondence on a day-to-day basis, as well as on a mammoth scale from time to time. Those who require the same quality but are involved in large mailings only every now and then, may use a *word processing bureau*. This type of application is one of the most frequently used services provided by such bureaux, who may offer a variety of services in addition to the use of word processors for typing clients' documents. These can include training, setting up new applications for customers who have their own equipment, provision of temporary staff, permanent staff recruitment, and even selling word processors and consumable items. And the larger bureaux tend to have access to a number of different types of machine.

Many *authors and journalists* have personally invested in equipment at the lower end of the market because of the need to continually redraft their work. Word processing has made this book possible! Without the facilities for preparing numerous drafts of the text, your authors would never have contemplated putting together such a work. Similarly, *engineer-*

ing and product support functions preparing lengthy and involved specifications or technical manuals that are continually being updated offer tremendous scope for word processing.

Publishing organisations or departments preparing newsletters, bulletins, or summaries that have to meet publication deadlines, yet are dependent on contributions from a variety of sources can derive significant benefits. *Financial departments* preparing statistical reports updated on a regular basis, with much of the data static and based on computer generated information that needs to be summarised and well presented for management, can use word processors linked to a corporate computer. Any business whose service involves communication via the written word is likely to make extensive use of word processing, since so often the same words appear in a variety of forms for a variety of clients or audiences. *Library and information services* fall into this category. They can use word processors to produce catalogues, indexes, bulletins, and in conjunction with information processing facilities for order processing, literature reference searching, maintenance of borrower records and journal circulation control.

But what about the other extreme? What type of organisation is unlikely to derive sufficient benefit to justify investment? If you produce a very small volume of unique documents, then it is highly unlikely that word processing will solve any problems you currently have or significantly increase efficiency or effectiveness in any way. Nonetheless, given word processing capabilities, there may be areas of opportunity to which you could extend your business. When combined with limited existing needs these could indeed lend enough weight to justify initial investment.

One aspect of prime importance and one that so often gets overlooked is to consider the likely *benefits to those responsible for originating documents*. In particular:-

1. Proof-reading time can be significantly reduced since only amendments need be checked (there being no need for complete retypes).

2. Document drafting time can be curtailed because standard paragraphs stored on

the system can be referred to by a code or number rather than cut-and-pasted into a manuscript by the originator.

③ Typists may be prepared to work from rough notes, knowing that later extensive editing or misinterpreted words can easily be corrected without complete retypes.

④ The quality of document content can improve significantly since originators no longer feel constrained by asking the typist to do another draft.

However, points (3) and (4) require considerable co-operation and understanding between originator and typist. Tolerance of poor scripts should not be taken for granted once word processing is installed, and originators need to learn to strike a balance between improving the quality of communications and polishing documents unnecessarily. But one manufacturing company has commented that, in the preparation of supporting technical documentation for their products "our writers have an inherent feel for what the word processor can do. They feel they can compose new text much more efficiently."

Checklist 1

We highlighted typical symptoms of problem situations in document preparation. If some have registered more than others, they could be the ones particularly close to home!

☐ managers doing work that could be done by secretaries;

☐ an unhappy secretarial and typing workforce;

☐ a high ratio of secretaries and typists to managers;

☐ frequent use of agency staff or excessive overtime;

☐ poor quality of typed output;

☐ document production deadlines not met, excessive turnround time;

☐ too much time spent in proof-correction.

The types of document that consistently show significant benefits from word processing are:

① Standard correspondence.

② Extensive revision required before editing.

③ Documents requiring first-class presentation.

④ Extensive use of standard sections of text.

⑤ Regular updates with some data or information static.

⑥ Sequenced lists.

⑦ Publication deadlines involved.

Most organisations are likely to be involved in at least one of these areas. Organisations or functions where benefits are readily identified include:

☐ the legal profession;

☐ sales and consultancy organisations;

☐ personnel functions;

☐ authors and journalists;

☐ engineering and product support functions;

☐ publishing organisations;

☐ financial departments;

☐ library and information services.

Remember to consider the likely benefits to document originators.

Word processing bureaux offer a variety of services.

Problem Analysis

Background – the word processing cycle

Origination
Production of the typed document
Reproduction
Distribution
Storage or filing

Background – document types

One-off correspondence (letters and memos)
Textual reports
Statistical reports and schedules
Lists
Repetitive correspondence and mail-shots
Proforma
Miscellaneous "documents"

Carrying out the analysis

Information to be gathered
Survey work

Checklist

Background – the word processing cycle

Analysis of your particular situation should firstly confirm that you would indeed benefit from word processing, and if so also identify the factors to be taken into account in ultimately selecting a system. You will need to look at the entire document production cycle, watching for signs of inefficiency, wasted or duplicated effort, and aggravation among employees.

Most managers and executives have only a vague idea of the volume and composition of their organisation's typing load. However, if decisions are to be made objectively it is critical for anyone responsible for identifying the desirable benefits, selecting equipment and assessing the ultimate gains, to have a clear understanding of this. It is possible that you will delegate much of the specific activity associated with this part of the exercise to a member of your staff, in which case the detail in this section is for them, but it is important that *you are also aware* of what is involved; so at the very least you are urged to scan the text.

We take you through the five steps in the cycle painting the picture as it is before word processing is installed. Bear in mind this is likely to be just the first step in the move towards automating the office, and one which should be taken with awareness of other areas to be tackled later. The cycle consists of:

1 Origination
2 Production of the typed document
3 Reproduction
4 Distribution
5 Storage or filing

Origination
What methods of document origination are there?

Shorthand, Speedhand or Stenography Dictation. This approach to first setting ideas or thoughts on paper is dependent on the mutual availability of the two people involved, the originator and the shorthand-typist. This must surely be to the detriment of recording fresh or inspired thoughts. The secretary has to wait while the originator pauses to think about what he or she is going to say or attends to an interruption. Similarly, the secretary may be interrupted, in which case the originator has to wait. It could be argued that such distractions should not be allowed to happen, but with the secretary occupied, it is unlikely that there is always someone else available to prevent them. However, this method does have the advantage of the personal approach.

Furthermore, provided the secretary's short-hand is good, the chances of producing accurate copy first time are higher than with other methods. But it is generally regarded as making inefficient use of people's time.

Machine Dictation. With this method the originator and typist can deal with the work according to their own routine and workload, the one is not dependent on the availability of the other. Potentially one of the most efficient ways of using people's time, much is dependent on:

□ the skills of the typist in audio work and of the originator in using dictating equipment;

□ the type, quality and availability of equipment – machines should be ready-to-hand, tapes should be compatible across machines and for urgent work the facility for transcription while dictation is taking place is essential;

□ procedures being established to deal with dictated work so that originators going off on long trips can have work dealt with while they are generating it, and typists are not presented with a load of tapes on the originator's return.

A disadvantage of this form of dictation, however, is the impersonal approach.

Long-hand. This tends to be the most frequently used method, particularly for work other than correspondence. It has the advantage again that the originator and typist can deal with the work according to their own routine and workload, and even more so than machine dictation, since it is not dependent on availability of equipment (other than the typewriter). It also has the advantage for the originator that they can read back their thoughts and instantly revise them. This method tends to be tedious for the typist who is slowed down by interpreting hand-writing, which can lead to the need for more corrections. Typists can be frustrated and feel abused by having to deal with poorly scripted work. The advantage is that no additional skills are required on the part of originator or typist.

Typed or Printed Material. This is likely to be the case when text or data is being incorporated from another source. Sometimes ma-

terial may be lifted from computer printout which is not one of the easiest sources for a typist to work from, as the printing is usually in upper case and paper size is awkward to handle.

Whatever the form of printed source, it is regrettable that having been "typed" or printed once already, effort is being duplicated in rekeying material.

Production of the Typed Document

We mentioned in the "Introduction" that the only prior knowledge assumed of readers was a basic understanding of typing tasks, but as already intimated, it is unlikely that all readers are aware of the sorts of *frustrations and sub-conscious decision-making* that a typist goes through. Consider:

1. Setting up a job entails the preparation of carbons (if needed), setting margins, tab-stops, spacing. And with tabular work the preparation in devising lay-out can be particularly time-consuming.

2. Errors can be generated by interruptions, lack of concentration, incomplete instructions, poor dictation, handwriting or manuscript presentation, hesitation about spelling, and the strain of trying to meet a deadline.

3. Even if the typist can cope with some of these difficulties without making errors, there will inevitably be a slowing down in typing speed.

4. Speed is further decreased by end-of-line decisions (will a word fit or not) and end-of-page decisions (should I start the next paragraph, will I be able to break the paragraph conveniently).

5. End-of-page productivity is further hampered by the additional care that the typist takes to avoid spoiling an otherwise perfect page.

6. With carbons each one has to be corrected.

7. If the typist decides to restart a page because of too many or complicated corrections, concentration is again interrupted, with scope for further errors.

8. To reduce the potential amount for retyping, typists tend to read through their work at the end of each paragraph. This in itself breaks concentration. It also means that mistakes are missed, as the tendency is to look at individual phrases or sentences, rather than a "communication of thoughts or ideas". This is why missing out complete sentences or paragraphs is always a possibility.

Having generated the first typed version, if retyping is necessary then many of the above hindrances to productivity still hold, but at least this time poorly presented manuscript is not a problem. Some originators, however, can be just as heavily criticised for the way they mark-up corrections as for the way they present original scripts. Alternatively, someone well versed in the art of dictation may leave much to be desired when amending typescript for correction. Although a perfectly good set of British Standards exists for marking proof-corrections, very few originators, typists or secretaries seem to be aware of these. Details are given in Appendix 1.

It is customary to type drafts in one-and-a-half or double line spacing leaving plenty of room for corrections. However, a retype may be needed for something that was thought, on the previous typing, to be a final copy and is therefore in single line spacing. In this case, the typist will probably be slower than working from a draft in one-and-a-half or double line spacing.

Reproduction

Producing multiple copies can be done in a variety of ways.

Carbon Copying. Carbon paper is used between the top copy and sheets of bank (flimsy), or paper pre-impregregnated with carbon is used. It is also possible to get "copysets" which come with the carbon attached to the flimsy. These and pre-impregnated paper have the advantage of being less fiddly to handle, but whatever the approach the disadvantage is that each carbon copy has to be corrected. This may be while the top paper plus copies are still in place, or after reinserting each copy into the typewriter, or correcting by hand. The maximum number of carbons that can reasonably be prepared using carbon paper is three, any more become fuzzy due to the lack of pressure through the paper. With impregnated paper, one or two more copies may reasonably be obtained.

Photocopying. This has the advantage that copying is not done until the final version of the document is ready, with only the top copy needing corrections applied. It tends to be more expensive than using carbons from the point-of-view of equipment and supply costs. These are offset by savings in staff time, unless a considerable amount of time is involved in walking to the copier. The copier itself is another piece of equipment and may therefore become unavailable due to break-down. Locally sited copiers mean that un-trained staff get faced with paper jamming and feeding problems or the need to load paper or top-up toner. Even if particular typists or secretaries are trained to do this, they may not always be available and the tendency is for staff to feel down-graded by having such responsibilities.

On the other hand if a central service is offered it may mean a delay before your job is done. However, additional facilities such as automatic collation, photo-reduction and "backing-up" (copying on both sides of the paper) may be offered.

Printing. Other methods of reproducing documents are by spirit or stencil-based duplicators. Such machines again require trained operators and the tendency these days is to offer offset-litho as a central service. The advantage of offset-litho is that the cost of reproduction is very low provided a minimum number of copies is being made (it can be as little as six) and the quality of reproduction can be very good. Additional facilities of

reduction, backing-up, collating and stapling are also likely to be offered as part of the service.

Distribution

Documents may be sent by internal mail, external post, facsimile transmission, special delivery service, or they may even be rekeyed for transmission by telex. Once received by the recipient they will either end up in the waste-paper bin or be filed, perhaps after an extended period in a pending or filing tray, or a manager's briefcase!

Storage or Filing

Each office tends to have its own system of storing material originated within the depart-ment. It is usually devised by the department's secretary and may or may not be based on recommendations laid down centrally.

A variety of problems are encountered with local filing systems.

1. A subjective rather than a logical, objective approach is used. This may be very good for the person doing most of the filing and retrieving, but it usually relies on memory and does not cater for the occasion when someone else has the filing or retrieving task.

2. Unless a checking-out system is devised, anyone can remove a file or set of papers and fail to return them.

3. Paper is bulky; so weeding needs to take place at regular intervals or continuously as new material is added, or else room allowed for expansion. Removing redundant papers can be time-consuming and tedious.

4. Microform (film, fiche or jacket) may be used to archive documents that have to be retained for a lengthy period and frees space. Although the process is relatively cheap, effort is required in getting material together ready for filming and in devising appropriate indexing to identify where a document is held in the microform. Reading equipment has to be made available with a possible option of being able to print pages on paper from the microform.

5 Several copies of a document will be filed in various locations within an organisation for ready access by each department's staff, which means filing effort is being duplicated.

Centralised filing systems or repositories require material to be organised by professional staff trained in how to store documents for later retrieval. Such people are able to devise good working systems based on the frequency of accessing documents, the need to cross-reference material, the need for precision in retrieving relevant documents, the comprehensiveness required in locating items concerning a particular topic, and the costs involved. However, no matter how efficient and reliable such a service is, individual offices will still want to hold their own copies of certain correspondence and other documents.

Background – document types

We have sketched the document processing cycle common within an office. We are now in a position to look at the types of document being generated and what is involved in their production, before going on to consider how to profile your complete workload.

One-off Correspondence (Letters and Memos)

These are usually contained in one or two pages and generally require a fast turnround. Retyping may be required to improve expression or to obtain high quality of presentation. The tendency is for such revisions not to be done when there is a heavy workload, or if it is, it may be under sufferance by the typist. The number of copies required varies from one to any number but usually is less than six.

Textual Reports

These may be progress reports, proposals, minutes of meetings, newsletters, bulletins, procedural documents, specifications, legal documents, job descriptions, brochures, or manuals. They may be anything from three to several hundred pages in length. Origination is usually in long-hand, a standard lay-out is specified to generate a consistent style for the documents if not a general house-style. They generally go through at least three revision cycles and there may be a deadline for each cycle. Revision may be the work of more than one person. Pages, if not the whole document, will have to be retyped.

Large quantities of "snopake" or similar blocking-out or correcting agent are probably used and sections may be cut-and-pasted to save retyping. Considerable time is spent not just in typing but proof-correction, since every section that is retyped will have to be proof-corrected. Reproduction is generally by photocopying or printing. The report may be a standard reference work that needs regular updating in which case the whole revision cycle has to be gone through each time. Or it may use standard sections of text brought together from previous reports and used time and time again.

Statistical Reports and Schedules

Budget statements, business forecasts, production and performance schedules are some examples. They can be anything from one to a number of pages in length. Origination is usually long-hand or marked-up typed or printed copy from another source. There is much lay-out work to be done and proforma may be used. Typing is slow because of the need to follow the lay-out, probably working within columns, and because figures or terse statements or descriptions rather than free-flowing text is used. Where figures are involved, accuracy is vital. Revisions tend to avoid retyping at all costs due to the effort required in generating the first version and the proof-correction required.

In instances where the report gets updated, a copy of the previous issue may be used and "snopaked" or cut-and-pasted to save retyping of static data. Often information is left out because of the difficulty and tediousness of altering the original format. For example, desirable footnotes may be excluded or information may be uncomprehendingly abbreviated because of limited space within a column. Data may be presented in segmented time-frames rather than on a "rolling-window" basis to avoid retyping previously reported figures. For example, a table for a weekly report may be set out to give up to four weeks data at a time. A new table is started every fifth week when the previous table is filled up. With a "rolling-window" approach, four weeks worth of figures are always reported, consisting of the previous three and the current week.

Lists

Usually these consist of a number of columns on a page even if only as continuations of a single column list. There may be figures involved. Typing may be a little tricky due to the need to contain overflow of items of information within columns, but generally not as involved as the schedules just mentioned. First typing generally serves also as the final copy with no retyping in the initial production stage. However, lists tend to be documents that are retained and updated which means that after a number of insertions, deletions and general revisions, a re-type with proof-correction is required. The information may also need to be held in a variety of sequences where all the entries have to be retyped for each version.

Lists tend to be tedious items to produce. If a strict sequence of entries has to be maintained this is often left to the typist to organise, or if not, the typist may be slowed down by watching for mistakes in the sequencing by the originator. Reproduction is generally by photocopying or printing. Lists can take the form of inventories and stock-lists, staff lists, telephone and other directories, customer and mailing lists, glossaries, library holdings, file headings, and catalogues.

Repetitive Correspondence and Mail-shots

Usually these are one page in length and fairly short. They may be the result of dictation, long-hand or completion of a form with details for personalising each version. If there is a minimum of difference between each one, such as an addressee change, pre-printed copies of the standard text may be used. This can then be topped (with addressee details and salutation) and perhaps also tailed (with a suitable closure) for each version. If a number of variables have to be incorporated in the text or the final output has to look totally personalised, then each letter will have to be individually typed.

If copies are required carbons are usually taken. The typist gets to know the text well, almost committing it to memory. Examples are letters of interview and appointment, contracts of employment, reminder letters, product announcements, letters canvassing for new custom, and responses to customer complaints.

Proforma

There are many instances in office work where proforma are used to ensure that all the information about a matter is recorded, such as invoices, purchase requisitions, claims, catalogue cards, and order forms. These may then be used as coding documents for data processing. Usually they are contained on one page. Origination is in long-hand, maybe even on a copy of the form. Forms may come in multiple-part sets. They are generally slow to complete because boxes, lines, and columns have to be lined up, accuracy is usually essential, and corrections have to be done to each carbon copy. Where a number of carbons are required, even a small number of mistakes after proof-correction may result in a new form being started and the data being completely re-typed, which is also expensive in stationery supplies.

Miscellaneous "Documents"

These can be cards of reference information (like business contacts), address labels, and file labels. All are fiddly in paper-handling, but generally are not difficult to type. Mailing labels may be typed time and time again for the same addressees over a period of time.

Carrying out the analysis

Information to be Gathered

The previous two sections discussed the production cycle and general categories of document with the characteristics of demands on the typist and originator or proof-corrector. You should now be in a position to think about the areas to be covered in profiling the workload of your own organisation. In looking at this and the symptoms of dissatisfaction with existing services, it should be possible to identify the cause of your problem(s). Bearing in mind our earlier summary of what word processors can do, you should also be able to decide whether word processing is a viable solution.

A reorganisation or enhancement of existing facilities may suffice. Providing adequate training for staff (typists and originators), arranging proper work-scheduling, being less demanding of quality for internal memos, sharing resources, allowing the use of hand-written documents instead of insisting on everything being typed, allowing flexibility in staff hours or requested overtime, or any combination of these may be the solution. Such alternatives should always be consi-dered first, for be assured, word processing – if it is to be used efficiently and effectively – will require just as much consideration and application with respect to training, proce-dures and office organisation.

What information needs to be gathered and analysed? There are many pieces of data that can usefully be collected. Any investigation should also be geared to providing informa-tion that will allow you to specify require-ments. The extent of the exercise will very much depend on:

- the overall objectives of contemplating word processing;

- how easy or difficult it is to gather the information (possibly involving internal politics, staff relationships, and trade unions); and

- availability of staff to carry out the exercise.

But at the very least, getting together a truly representative sample of the workload will require some study. However, we caution you against finalising any survey or investiga-tion until you have covered the remaining parts of the book, grasped the extent of facilities available and fully appreciate the potential benefits to your organisation.

Document Production Profile. There are a variety of questions that need to be answered.

The Typing Load:

1. How much time is spent by staff typing?

2. What is the break-down in terms of type of origination (long-hand, short or speed-hand, audio, typed, computer printout)? This is relevant to later questions on frustrations and difficulties in dealing with originators' work and in examining the source of material that has already been keyed.

3. How many pages of top copy are generated on average a week (ignore carbon copies made)? This is needed together with questions (1) and (4) to calculate potential increases in productivity and the ultimate workload to be catered for.

4. What types of documents are produced and specifically, how much of the work (number of pages and time involved if possible):

    - requires complete retypes because of revision or updating;

    - is composed of standard text;

    - is tabular or involves lists;

    - uses proforma;

    - involves amending previous issues of typed documents?

Note these are not mutually exclusive. The amount of time spent and number of pages involved in dealing with each of these parts of the workload are important. For example, a typist could spend many hours typing proforma but deal with many pages in the time because these are short and relatively straightforward. Word processing would be unlikely to prove a significant advantage to the typing effort in this case. Or a relatively long time per page of retyping suggests extensive editing which may still take a significant amount of time on a word processor.

5. What proportion of the work (typing time):

    - requires first-class presentation;

    - involves publication deadlines or tight timescales;

    - is confidential, and what security measures are needed?

Again these are not mutually exclusive. The figures will give an indication of the extent to which staff work under pressure and security requirements of the system ultimately chosen.

6. Are there any documents or jobs that currently pose problems or limitations? What are they? Word processing may get round the problem.

7 What are the major difficulties and sources of frustration for typists? It could be technical jargon, difficulties in interpreting orginators' long-hand, tight timescales. Word processing may make a significant contribution to surmounting these.

8 What is the pattern of peaks and troughs in the typing workload? What causes them? Word processing may allow these to be smoothed as work can begin on documents before drafting is complete. If peaks are still likely to occur these will need to be catered for in determining the overall capacity of a system.

9 How much additional effort is required using agency typing staff? Again this will have to be taken into account in determining overall capacity. The expenditure involved may help to justify investment in equipment if permanent staff productivity can be increased sufficiently to eliminate the need for agency staff.

Printing and Reproduction:

1 What levels of preprinted stationery are used – memo, letter-head, proforma and others? To what extent, if any, is multi-part stationery used and what is required in the way of envelope addressing? This is required to determine the approach to feeding stationery into the printer which may result in additional investment.

2 How many copies of each document are required and how are these produced? This can be used in evaluating the benefits of continuing to take carbons, using the word processor to print multiple top copies of documents, or photocopying.

It is important to also determine whether any of these patterns are likely to change over the next two years. There is no good planning to improve today's situation if tomorrow's is likely to be very different!

A few questions to test staff's reaction to the potential for word processing may also help to identify current problem areas. They could be asked to state what they see as the main benefits, if any, from their understanding of what word processing is. This could provide you with a further opportunity of assessing people's enthusiasm.

The preceding questions will give you a profile of the current document production workload and an indication of anticipated changes. Also important are questions that identify other responsibilities of typing staff and how these relate to the typing load when it comes to priorities, number of staff serviced and responsibility levels.

System Replacement. Systems based on earlier technology such as magnetic card or tape may be in use within the organisation. This will need to be taken into account in planning replacement with equipment based on newer technology, as material held on card or tape will need to be converted to the new equipment.

Originator Activity. It is important to get a measure of the time originators spend in proof-correcting and the proportion of this that involves dealing with completely retyped work. There may also be instances of documents not getting typed that should be, and as a result are either never distributed, or are sent to other staff who then take twice as long to read them because of poor hand-writing.

Pre and Post Stages. What happens to the typed output? Is it processed further or rekeyed for any reason? Could you use some of the additional facilities offered – for example linking to a larger computer, other word processors or the telex network? Conversely, if material is other than original thought, examine the source. There may be scope for taking the information straight from its original source if in magnetic form and editing it for your document requirements. Or if it requires manipulation before typing, the processes gone through should be analysed. These may include sorting or calculations that could possibly be done by the system.

Survey Work
In larger organisations the information will probably have to be gathered by questionnaires that staff complete on their own. With this approach, the time spent preparing questions and testing them out on staff will be well rewarded in gathering useful and reliable information from the real exercise. In a small department or business it may be sufficient to devise an appropriate checklist to be worked

through with staff.

All staff involved should at the very least be thoroughly briefed as to why the exercise is being carried out. It is vital that staff are dealt with honestly and that time is taken to explain what word processors can do plus the potential benefits. Stress the important role staff have to play in providing this information and that exact figures are not being sought, estimates will suffice. What you require is an overall picture of average throughput based on a typical working fortnight or month, with scope for highlighting peaks and troughs. Where unions are present, we have already suggested it is wise to involve them fully.

To assist typists in answering questions, it may help to design a form they can use to monitor the workload over the specified period. Some organisations ask typists to take an extra copy of everything they do during the investigation, so that the extent of revisions, page lengths and complicated lay-outs can be examined. This adds to the thoroughness of the exercise, provided someone has time to analyse the copies!

The analysis should allow you to decide whether word processing is likely to be a worthwhile investment. And you should have the basis for selecting particular equipment to suit your needs.

Checklist 2

The "word processing" cycle covers:

1. Origination.
2. Production of the typed document – typists are exposed to a variety of frustrations and sub-conscious decision-making.
3. Reproduction.
4. Distribution.
5. Storage or filing.

Documents can be categorised as:

- one-off correspondence (letters and memos);
- textual reports;
- statistical reports and schedules;
- lists;
- repetitive correspondence and mail-shots;
- proforma;
- miscellaneous.

Carrying Out The Analysis: The following sets of data are recommended for consideration in profiling document production.

The typing load:

1. Total typing time.
2. Type of document origination.
3. Total number of pages typed.
4. Document types and proportion of the typing load.
5. Requirements for good presentation, meeting deadlines, confidential typing.
6. Jobs with problems or limitations.
7. Difficulties and frustrations for typists.
8. Peaks and troughs.
9. Use of agency staff.

Printing and reproduction:

1. Use of preprinted stationery.
2. Number of copies made.

Determine also the future changes anticipated.

These need to be supplemented by information about originator time in proof-correction, current use of magnetic card or tape systems, where the information contained in the document comes from, and what subsequently happens to it.

In larger organisations a questionnaire survey will probably be required to collect the necessary data. In small departments or businesses a checklist to be worked through with staff may suffice.

Management and Organisational Issues

System types

Stand-alone dedicated word processors
Shared logic systems
Distributed logic/intelligence or information
processing systems
Shared resource systems
Software packages on computer systems

Organisation of word processing services

Centralisation
Decentralisation
Management responsibilities for a word
processing function

Selecting and installing a system

Commitment
Personnel issues
The suppliers
Equipment selection activities
Preparation for installation

Checklist

Chapter 3 is concerned with major management issues in installing word processing equipment. It covers the way word processing services can be arranged within an organisation and project management of equipment selection and installation. But before these can be discussed we first need to describe the different types of system available.

System types

Word processing systems fall into five major categories although these are by no means absolute or mutually exclusive.

Stand-Alone Dedicated Word Processors

Stand-alone means the processor (together with internal memory), screen, keyboard, printer and external storage are all part of the workstation used by the typist, whom we shall now refer to as the operator. Dedicated means that the system is first and foremost used for word processing and related applications. Such systems are the major product line of many suppliers and will also feature within the product range of those who concentrate on larger systems.

Stand-alone dedicated word processors may be no more than an electronic typewriter with the keyboard and printer as integral units and with no more than a one line display. Some may not even have an external storage medium or memory, but instead have a significant amount of internal memory. The "word processing" capabilities of electronic typewriters may be limited in comparison with the type of systems on which this book concentrates, but their lower cost and relative ease of operation have given them a role in the market-place as we previously indicated.

Shared Logic Systems

In this case a number of workstations share the processor, external storage and printing facilities. Workstations are usually connected to the shared facilities via cable but it can be via a telephone line. Processing power is significantly greater than in a stand-alone system. Each terminal has a keyboard and screen. If the central processor ceases to work then the terminals, referred to as "dumb terminals", cannot work. Some processors can handle over 30 workstations but somewhere between 8 and 16 is more common.

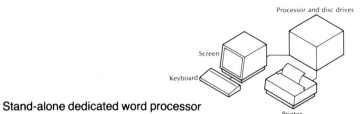

Stand-alone dedicated word processor

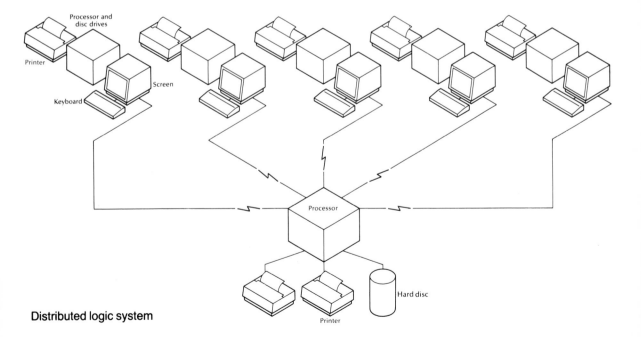

Shared logic system

Distributed logic system

Shared logic systems have the advantage of economies of scale, and tend to be more suited to central typing pool environments where partitioning of responsiblities is characteristic. With such a system someone needs to be responsible for control of the central processor and the printers.

Distributed Logic/Intelligence or Information Processing Systems

Here also the workstations are linked to the central processor of a larger computer via cables or telephone lines. However, each station (which is also likely to have its own printer) can work independently. The logic or software which can be transmitted via a communications link, is dispersed to the terminals when the system is first switched on for the day (sometimes referred to as downline loading). Or a separate copy of the software may be held on disc at the workstation since there will also be local external storage facilities. However, when necessary these systems can access the main computer for documents, data, and software for additional applications.

Because the word processing software is held locally on the machine, such systems do not become inoperable when the main computer goes down. Workstations here are referred to as "smart" or "intelligent terminals". Such systems are really a marriage between word processing and data processing.

Shared Resource Systems

Whenever an independent workstation or the terminal of a distributed logic system shares another piece of equipment such as disc storage, greater processing power or a printer, a shared resource system is established. It may simply be two or more independent stations sharing a printer or floppy disc drives, or it may be a stand-alone system temporarily linked to a shared logic system for increased processing power.

Software Packages on Computer Systems

Word processing software packages are available to run on micros, minis or mainframe computers as just one of the applications run on the system. There are many such packages available with a few having become particularly well established in the last year or so. Of

particular note are those that run under the CP/M operating system (Control Program for Microcomputers). The operating system is the software that controls the computer. It organises reading from and writing to discs, communicating with a printer and VDU, maintaining records of where information is stored, and so on. CP/M is designed to run on a variety of microcomputers and a wealth of applications software has been written for it. It has become known as a "de facto" software standard for the microcomputing industry.

Organisation of word processing services

The arrangement of word processing services within an organisation may influence system selection. If a centralised typing pool is to be provided with equipment or established as the result of introducing word processing, then a shared or distributed logic system may be viable. If decentralised typing services are involved, stand-alone systems may be more appropriate. If you are concerned with only a small business or a small department within a larger organisation, you may like to skip this section and move on to "Selecting and Installing a System".

Centralisation

In the early days of word processing systems the tendency was to install these and create word processing centres using shared logic systems. The reasons were:

☐ the equipment was a new innovation and therefore required staff to be trained from scratch;

☐ systems were relatively expensive (several times the annual salary of an operator) so that maximum use was sought by having highly skilled operators and by making the facilities available to a variety of departments within an organisation; and

☐ the early equipment tended to be best suited to applications associated with a highly productive typing workload, in particular repetitive work (unlike most day-to-day secretarial applications), and these were generally associated with a typing pool environment.

Centralisation of word processing applications can still be a practical and viable approach but it has *disadvantages*. A number are often cited.

1. Operators feel cut off from the people supplying the work and may not be responsible for a job from start to finish. This can affect staff morale with the resultant impact on the quality of work done.

2. Limited communications between originator and operator and lack of familiarity with the work can lead to more editing being required, which in turn can result in lowering the standard of output. People begin to lose interest if a document goes through one draft after another.

3. Problems can arise in staff relationships within the centre between operators, but more commonly between operators and their supervisor.

4. Staff progression may be limited.

5. Centralisation may mean the loss of personal secretaries for some managers.

6. Certain administrative procedures may need to be introduced for the use of the centre and this can lead to an unfriendly image.

7. Physical separation of the centre from the departments it serves may discourage people from using it, as well as promote an unfriendly and aloof image.

8. Work can soon take on a repetitive production line profile leading to operator fatigue and morale problems.

But run well and in the right environment *a word processing centre can prove an efficient and effective solution* for document preparation activities. In particular, where:

- it is highly desirable to have the scope offered by shared or distributed logic systems for using greater processing power, as well as more advanced facilities and applications software;

- applications require highly skilled operators working closely with originators to make extensive use of some of the more sophisticated facilities;

- it is cost-effective for the organisation to share a number of workstations and operators across a variety of departments and staff;

- centralisation is justified on the basis of offering an entire range of pooled services from audio dictation to reproduction.

To make such a set-up work, however, depends on finding the correct formula covering organisation, work design, environment, the right staff, and training provision. The overall aim must be to generate good relationships within the centre as well as between it and the departments serviced, and this includes direct contact between originators and operators.

Extending the range of services seems to have worked for some organisations since this has had a beneficial effect on individuals' responsibilities, scope, flexibility and ultimate job satisfaction. In particular, some companies have gone for a secretarial rather than just a word processing centre, where secretaries, clerks and operators work together as a team, all being capable to some extent of using the equipment. Each person services a number of managers and staff, but there is provision for spreading the workload in peak situations or staff absence. Other organisations have succeeded by providing scope for developing the operator role through the use of additional software on the system(s); in particular, communication with larger computers and responsibilities for database update and interrogation, as well as carrying out computer applications on behalf of a group of managers and staff.

Decentralisation
Many companies that were some of the original investors in word processing have now allowed decentralisation of equipment, or have permitted individual installations in addition to continued running of a centre. This has been brought about by a relative decrease in the price of equipment, the introduction of systems that are easier to learn, and the increase in population of staff with some word processing experience. Also significant is the increasing emphasis on cost-effectiveness of managers and executives with the need for more closely assigned support staff. This is especially so now that

additional applications software is becoming available to run on stand-alone systems.

Decentralisation is considered viable in organisations where the secretary or typist is required to understand the jargon of a particular department or type of work, where most of the work requires a fast turnround, or where many other duties have to be performed. It may be mandatory where management and executives require the back-up that secretaries can provide in spotting inconsistencies and even "bloomers" in the work they are asked to type. Secretaries may be depended upon to use their initiative in deciding how to lay out documents to suit the originator, or in constructing routine or brief letters on behalf of management.

Decentralised arrangements need not use stand-alone equipment, distributed logic systems may be suitable. Arrangements can also involve the sharing of a system by a number of departments provided someone has ultimate responsibility for the day-to-day running of the system. Decentralisation provides scope for development of the managerial workstation as the next step in the automated office, with local stations having the facility for communication with each other, a main computer, or other items of electronic equipment and used for other routine business activities.

Management Responsibilities for a Word Processing Function

In organisations installing shared or distributed logic systems, or where a number of stand-alone word processing systems are to be installed, decisions may need to be taken to allocate the overall responsibility for word processing within the organisation. Responsibilities to be covered may include:

□ equipment selection;

□ installation;

□ preparation of job descriptions;

□ staff selection and training;

□ maintenance and in-house support to help in problem situations, to advise on new applications and system enhancements, and to liaise with the supplier;

□ identification of new departments requiring word processing facilities;

□ preparation of guidelines and procedures;

□ bulk ordering of consumables;

□ evaluation of existing installations.

Responsibilities may be allocated within the data processing department, office administration function, or organisation-and-methods department. The exercise may provide the opportunity for a re-think of existing corporate structure and the establishment of a new function embracing all the company's information resources – data processing, telecommunications, office services, and libraries. Given the convergence of office equipment towards the establishment of the "automated office", this approach is increasingly being adopted by large companies.

Selecting and installing a system

Commitment

If your system is to succeed, it will require commitment: commitment from those (if other than yourself) who have to sanction the capital expenditure and who must be prepared to accept any major organisational changes needed to make it a success. And commitment will be required, to the extent of thorough involvement, from the person with direct responsibility for the system.

The application of word processing to an organisation's workload should be exciting and rewarding but success is also dependent on the contributions and collaboration of its people. It is vital that from the outset those involved or affected by the installation are assured of:

□ the commitment from top management;

□ the benefits to be derived;

□ job security and scope for job development; and

□ the need for their participation.

There are a number of ways that can contribute towards achieving this.

1 Be seen to pay attention to the personnel issues.

2 Establish a familiarisation programme (suggestions are given in Chapter 11).

③ Make the exercise the subject of a formal project with a project leader and representatives from all sections involved – secretaries and typists, originators, managers, personnel, office administration, training, and if appropriate trade unions.

④ Delegate responsibilities concerned with equipment selection and installation.

⑤ Base decisions on the information gathered and the recommendations of those involved.

⑥ Once equipment has been installed provide a forum for discussion of progress and problems.

⑦ Ensure that top management are seen to be making use of the new facilities.

These activities are just as relevant to small businesses as to large companies and government establishments.

Personnel Issues

Once over the initial fears and mis-apprehensions most staff find they prefer using a word processor to the typewriter because of:

□ the ease with which accurate and well-formatted documents can be produced;

□ removal of the tedious and unsatisfactory methods of altering documents with correcting paper and fluids or by cutting-and-pasting;

□ removal of repetitive typing;

□ the scope for taking pride in their work through improved presentation;

□ the challenge of using new equipment; and

□ the opportunity to learn new skills.

However, there are a few staff who are unable to accept the increased reponsibility and never settle to becoming good operators. Such people should not be forced to conform. Others will ask to be trained and then leave to sell their newly acquired skills elsewhere. Some demand regrading because of their additional skills. Some secretaries and personal assistants remain opposed to learning because they look on an activity that essentially involves keyboarding as downgrading, or else they fear an additional workload as a result of learning to use the equipment.

Such attitudes need to be anticipated and handled in conjunction with your personnel organisation. New job descriptions should certainly be prepared, appropriate salary gradings examined and career paths possibly restructured. It is no good leaving these personnel issues to wait and see whether any demands are made for new job titles and regrading. Be aware that others have adopted this approach and regretted it, because staff crises have resulted and in some cases industrial relations situations have developed.

Staff responsibilities and attributes to be looked for in selecting and appointing staff are covered in more detail in Chapters 10 and 11, with information provided on which job descriptions can be based. Career paths may take the line of trainee operator, operator, senior operator, and supervisor responsible for the day-to-day running of the system(s). As we intimated earlier, in large organisations the role of word processing manager responsible for a number of systems may need to be introduced. As office automation develops within an organisation responsibilities for using other electronic equipment may provide scope for staff progression.

The Suppliers

There are now well over 100 companies manufacturing word processing equipment. Many more are selling it. Although we described five major types of system, those now being developed are more difficult to categorise in this way and some systems can be upgraded so that they change from one category to another. A number of newcomers to the market-place are packaging together the equipment and the software and offering these as a system, marketing it under their own name. In 1976 suppliers were striving to offer equipment below £10,000 per workstation. By mid-1982 the price for most dedicated, stand-alone systems being introduced started at just under £4,000 (for the basics), but the costs of acquiring and installing a system are covered in much greater detail in Chapter 12.

Suppliers include the large multinational

computer manufacturers who have added office automation equipment to their list of products, mini and microcomputer manufacturers, companies who specialise in word processors and related products, office equipment dealers, software houses (companies who specialise in writing software usually tailored to individual customers' needs), word processing bureaux, and now shops. The company may be the manufacturer, an agent or dealer for another supplier, they may package together one manufacturer's hardware with their own or another company's software, or act merely as a retail outlet. For those specialising in just word processing and related equipment, you may find that they are part of a much larger organisation operating in an entirely different field.

Systems marketed in the UK are likely to have been made in this country, the States, or Japan. Where a supplier is merely marketing someone else's system they may dress it up in their own casing and/or label and may even have customised the system for their own market. Some of the well-established system suppliers in mid-1982 were AES Data, CPT, Data Recall, IBM, ICL, Monotype Communications, Philips, Rank Xerox, Wang, and Wordplex. There are many many more. Word processing packages for micros include Wordstar to run on machines with the CP/M operating system, Wordcraft to run on CBM Commodore PET machines, and Scripsit for Tandy microcomputers. Again there are many more. And there are packages to run on a variety of mini and mainframe computers of suppliers such as Data General, DEC (Digital Equipment Corporation), Honeywell and Hewlett Packard.

A further point to bear in mind is that in putting together a system, with a few notable exceptions including IBM, Wang and Olivetti, manufacturers do not to make the printers themselves but rely on the products of companies such as Qume, Diablo, Ricoh, and NEC (Nippon Electric Company). Again the supplier may or may not put the equipment in their own casing and/or label.

Equipment Selection Activities
Much will depend on the set-up and allocation of responsibilities within individual organisations. The requirement may be for a system to service a small business or just one department within a large company. It may be a system shared across a number of departments, or alternatively, a number of systems may be needed for a variety of functions within the organisation. Some companies will have no word processing experience to call on, others may employ one or two staff who have used word processing elsewhere. We recommend nine major steps to be followed, with the prime objective of increasing your chances of success in choosing and installing equipment.

We again draw attention to the importance of ensuring that the staff involved have been briefed about what is happening and that their co-operation and contributions are encouraged by way of criticisms and suggestions. We suggested earlier that establishing a formal project with a project leader and representatives of all involved was one way of getting commitment from people. Alternatively, an external consultant can be commissioned to assist with the exercise. Consultants have the advantage of being totally objective and they have considerable background knowledge and experience in the subject. Assistance offered can include the initial investigation, equipment selection, planning the installation of the system, organising staff training, staff selection and workload conversion. Consultants must be independent of any supplier or at least any affiliation should be clearly stated.

1. Firstly, carry out *an analysis* as outlined in Chapter 2 to determine whether you need word processing equipment, and to profile the applications and workload mix that you want to use it for. Then define precisely the benefits you are seeking. It is important to keep this profile and your expectations clearly in mind throughout the selection process.

2. Find out what *existing computing or word processing* facilities are potentially available to you. It may be feasible to run a word processing package on one of your computer systems, or you may want to use an existing word processing site as back-up to your own.

3. Prepare a *specification* of the system requirements and identify: (a) the

mandatory features; (b) those less vital but potentially useful; and (c) those where a possible use is envisaged but only as later developments in your applications. The specification should also cover number of systems required, any budget constraints and what you require in the way of support (including maintenance and training), later system enhancement and delivery dates. It is unlikely that you will find one system to perfectly match your needs. It is more likely you will have to decide on the design compromises most acceptable to you.

4. Select a representative *sample* of the workload to discuss and try out with prospective suppliers.

5. Carry out some *desk research* to familiarise yourself with the suppliers, their products, their marketing and pricing policies. This can be done by reading review articles and directories as well as talking to colleagues who already have equipment. Appendix 1 gives further sources of information to help you in this stage. Then narrow the field of potential suppliers.

6. Attend appropriate exhibitions (see Appendix 1) and contact suppliers for *literature* and to arrange *demonstrations*. In attending these, do not be fobbed off with slick sales talk, nor be afraid to ask many detailed questions about the way the system carries out its tasks, and questions beginning "what happens if …?". Do persist with getting your work samples done, watching how the jobs are set up and processed, and how easy, difficult, or involved this appears.

7. Prepare a *short-list* of suppliers.

8. Contact or if possible *visit existing customers*. There is a danger in asking suppliers for names of customers who may be approached, as the supplier is likely to recommend only those who can be relied upon to say nice things. If possible ask for a sizeable list and make your own choice of whom to contact.

9. Examine *suppliers' standard contracts and begin negotiations* over terms and conditions.

In respect of point (6), competent demonstrators or support staff (rather than sales people) are usually happy to discuss the intricacies of the system with you and welcome the opportunity to test their knowledge in more depth than is normally required at demonstrations. Support staff also tend to be more down to earth in discussing the system's capabilities, how it can be applied to your specific tasks, and to explain any jargon you might not understand. It may be worth insisting that such a person be available, or at least on call, during the demonstration. Ensure also that suppliers have allowed time for hands-on trial by you or your staff.

While all this is going on you may wish to try out some applications using one of the increasing number of word processing bureaux becoming established. Or it may be that as a result of analysing the situation you decide the time is not quite right to invest in your own equipment, but it is justifiable to use a bureau for a number of applications. However, you should bear in mind that once you do acquire your own equipment, it may be totally incompatible with that used by the bureau. Work already held on disc may have to be rekeyed unless suitable conversion facilities exist.

With the wealth of suppliers and options available it is vital to define your needs and profile your requirements in the manner we have suggested. It may be that in coming face-to-face with different equipment, you will realise further potential application areas or change your mind about the importance of certain features. Be prepared to revise your specification and to return to a supplier and ask more questions. However, do bear in mind that it is pointless to pay for features that you will hardly ever use, or for those that are desirable yet so complicated to implement that they will never be used by your staff.

Preparation for Installation
While specification of requirements and selection of equipment is taking place, planning and effort also needs to be devoted to preparation for installing the chosen system. The people affected may cover only a handful of staff in your own small business or office, or it may be a number of personnel across a variety of departments within a large com-

pany. Devoting significant care and attention to the "people" issues concerning the day-to-day operation of a system will ease the introduction of word processing technology into any office. Much of Part III is devoted to these. Many of the decisions on points of detail can be delegated to appropriate staff, but success from the managerial point-of-view requires a sound appreciation of the issues involved.

You should be aware of:

☐ what needs to be done to achieve smooth running of the system and to help staff make the most of its capabilities; and

☐ how to capitalise on the potential for job satisfaction, not just for those closely involved with the operation of the system, but those who will benefit from it as a means of "processing their words".

Checklist 3

Systems fall into five major categories:

☐ stand-alone dedicated word processors;

☐ shared logic systems;

☐ distributed logic/intelligence or information processing systems;

☐ shared resource systems;

☐ software packages on computer systems.

Centralisation of word processing services may be viable in a larger organisation where:

☐ greater processing power as well as more advanced facilities and applications software are desirable;

☐ highly skilled operators are required;

☐ it is cost-effective to share facilities across departments;

☐ a range of pooled services can be offered.

Decentralisation is viable where:

☐ typists are required to understand jargon;

☐ fast turnround is needed;

☐ many other duties have to be performed;

☐ secretarial back-up is required for managers and executives.

Decisions may need to be taken about allocating overall responsibility for word processing within a larger organisation.

If your system is to succeed it will require commitment.

Personnel Issues: anticipate staff attitudes, devote attention to job descriptions, salary regradings, and structuring career paths.

Suppliers cover a variety of business categories and backgrounds from manufacturers to agents, dealers and shops, from multinationals to small local word processing bureaux, from those purely in the business of office automation to furniture suppliers, oil companies, or whatever. A significant amount of repackaging and dressing up of alternatively sourced equipment takes place.

Nine steps are recommended in selecting equipment:

1. Analyse your situation, profiling the workload and defining the benfits sought.

2. Find out about existing computing and word processing facilities in the organisation.

3. Prepare a specification of system requirements.

4. Select a representative workload sample.

5. Do desk research to familiarise yourself with products and the market-place.

6. Attend exhibitions, collect literature and arrange demonstrations.

7. Prepare a short-list.

8. Contact or visit existing customers.

9. Examine suppliers' contracts and start negotiating.

In the meantime also start preparing for installation and above all, pay attention to the "people" issues!

PART II
Equipment Selection

Our aim in Part II is to provide details of the facilities and features offered by systems and to comment on a number of other matters relevant to equipment selection. Coupled with an analysis of the type discussed in Part I, you should then be in a position to specify requirements and to compare what suppliers have to offer. We cannot be comprehensive in describing all the options. We are more concerned with helping you to realise the sorts of variations possible and why these should be looked at when evaluating equipment. In the "Introduction" we suggested that if you have not already seen a word processor in operation, then you should try and do so before attempting to cover the detail in Part II. We believe you will get more out of it as a result.

Chapter 4 discusses the hardware, the equipment itself as opposed to the software. Chapter 5 covers software, the computer programs or intelligence that make it all work. It concentrates on the basic features expected of equipment and their ease of use.

Many suppliers now provide a number of extra facilities to further aid the typist and author or document originator, such as spelling checks and sorting lists into sequence. Those commonly on offer are discussed in Chapter 6 where communication links and compatibility are also covered.

Chapter 7 deals with support matters. These are also key factors in selecting equipment, as is supplier reputation.

A variety of consumable items are required by word processing equipment. Such items affect cost considerations, as does the scope in being able to fit ancillary equipment to the printer for paper handling and noise reduction. These matters are covered in Chapter 8.

No matter what the problem is that you are seeking to resolve, one of the most exciting aspects about word processing is that having dealt with the immediate problem, those who install equipment successfully will find new application areas leading to even greater rewards. You are therefore urged to keep an open mind about what is offered, in order to realise other uses to which equipment might be put within your organisation.

Hardware

Visual display

How a CRT works
Screen size
Colour and contrast
Character design
The cursor
Screen text movement
Screen manoeuverability
Split screen working

Keyboard

General ergonomics
Function and control keys
Additional facilities

Printer

Daisywheel printer
Spinwriter
Golf-ball printers
Dot matrix printers
Ink-jet printers
Factors for evaluation
Some general points

The processor and storage

The processor
Internal storage – the memory
External storage – floppy discs
External storage – hard discs

Checklist

Visual display

The visual display unit, also referred to as VDU, VT (video terminal), CRT (cathode ray tube), screen or simply display, is made up of four major parts. These are: a screen for the display of information; a control unit; a communications module providing circuits required to send and receive information to and from other equipment; and a keyboard for the entry of text, data or instructions. The first three are housed in a metal, fibreglass or plastic unit equipped with an internal fan and ventilation slits to help reduce the heat. The keyboard may be integrated with the housing unit or connected to the screen via a short cable.

There are a number of characteristics of the display screen that contribute towards ease of use of a system and to operator efficiency. These include the size of screen and the amount of information displayed, how information is displayed, and how easy it is for the operator to relate what is on the screen to the printed page. This section of Chapter 4 is devoted to these issues. Similar aspects about the keyboard are covered in a separate section. Some of the points about operator comfort are discussed further in Chapter 9.

How a CRT Works

The CRT is an evacuated glass tube with an electron gun at one end and a screen coated with light emitting material (phosphor) at the other. When a high electrical voltage is supplied to the gun, a stream of electrons is produced and focused into a narrow beam. The beam can be directed to any position on the CRT screen. When the beam strikes the phosphor coating the electrons interact with the phosphor and cause the phosphor grains to glow. The result is a bright spot on the screen. The type of phosphor used varies. Examples are P31 giving a green spot and P4 white.

Each character is designed as a series of small dots within a defined matrix. To display the character a bright spot is generated at each specified dot position (and at the required line and column position on the screen). The pattern of dots for each character is stored in a memory within the VDU. When a particular character is required (for example as the result of a keystroke on the keyboard), relevant information is retrieved from the memory and used to control the generation of spots on the screen.

There are other forms of character generation used in VDU's but the approach described is the one commonly used for word processing systems and microcomputers.

Screen Size
There are three main sizes of screen according to the number of lines accommodated – *quarter, half, or full (A4) page displays.* Quarter covers anything from as little as 6 lines of text to about 16; half, which is the most common, gives around 22 – 24 lines; and full-page can be anywhere between 50 and 70 lines. (There are exceptions to these three categories.) Full-page displays are useful for documents involving complicated lay-outs and provide additional help in relating what is being typed to the page eventually printed out. However, if page endings (boundaries) are clearly displayed on the screen and it is possible to move the text vertically through the display area (like a page advances through a typewriter), so that the end of one page and the beginning of the next can be viewed together, then operators quickly get used to smaller than full-page displays. This facility is known as scrolling and is discussed in more detail in Chapter 5.

Screen size is also defined by the number of characters or columns accommodated across the screen. This is usually 80 but a few systems provide well over 100. Since *80 columns* or less are used on an A4 page (in 10 or 12 pitch which are commonly used in office typing), this width of screen is easy to work with and the norm for dedicated word processors. However, anyone whose workload involves a significant proportion of tables or schedules requiring a greater line width than 80 characters may be better advised to opt for a system with a wider screen. On cheaper micro systems where word processing is just one of the software packages offered, screens were initially as small as 40 columns wide and totally unsuitable for any significant amount of word processing use. But nearly all newer models of micros now offer at least 60 and very often 80 columns.

Some screens provide the facility for looking at much larger areas of the document than are normally displayed. For example the number of lines displayed when keying in and editing text might be 22, but on command the system will reduce the size of the displayed characters and present the equivalent of an A4 page to help visual effect in checking lay-out. Some can even display a full A3 page in this way.

When talking about number of lines displayed we deliberately quoted number of lines of text. But an additional two to five lines may be provided at the top and/or bottom of the screen for use by the system to display control information helpful to the operator. These are referred to as the *scale or ruler line* and *status, prompt, or message lines.*

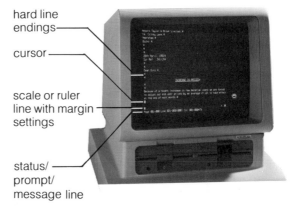

hard line endings

cursor

scale or ruler line with margin settings

status/ prompt/ message line

Control information – Wordplex 80-3

The following information may be included in these system lines.

1. Information about the document being worked on such as disc and document reference or name, and the current line and column position the operator is at.

2. Particular facilities being used at the time and usually referred to as functions, commands or modes. A typical example is when the operator is working in underline mode where all characters typed will be underlined.

3. Prompts to remind the operator of an action they need to take, or to generally guide them through an operation a step at a time. For example, on requesting deletion of a piece of text, the system may first prompt the operator to specify the text to be deleted, then follow this with an instruction to activate deletion.

4. A scale or ruler line identifying line width of the document, margin settings, tab stops, and perhaps the centre point of the typing line. The scale line may also identify the horizontal co-ordinates (column position) of where the typist has reached and the next character will be typed.

5. Error or warning messages from the system to perhaps alert the operator to an invalid command or a more serious situation.

Systems may also offer a "help facility" where considerably more information can be displayed on demand to explain particular functions.

This **control information** is particularly helpful to the operator. It therefore needs to be displayed so that it can be monitored readily but without distracting the flow of operations, except in the case of critical error messages. Some suppliers will quote total number of characters to define screen size but lines and columns are more meaningful to most people in thinking about the printed page. Physical dimensions quoted for screens generally include the length of the diagonal, 12 inches is common.

Colour and Contrast
Screens are usually one of the following:

- white or green or amber characters on a black or grey background;
- light green characters on a dark green background;
- black characters on a white background.

Some systems allow the operator to choose for example between black on white or white on black for normal working. To identify sections of a document to which particular commands are being applied (like moving a block of text), **highlighting facilities** are available. This may be by dimming the rest of the screen compared with the relevant text, a reverse video facility, or causing the characters to flash or blink. Reverse video means that the opposite of the normal mode of working takes effect, e.g. if the norm is green

on black, the reverse video will be black on green. Screen flashing can be a source of annoyance to the operator and reverse video can make screen flickering more perceptible.

Much has been written about VDU safety and ergonomics. Ergonomics is the study of the efficiency of workers and working arrangements. Radiation and eyestrain are the two areas of prime concern. Research by various professional bodies has confirmed that VDU's are not harmful from emitted radiation. Eyestrain is more likely to occur in operators already having uncorrected vision defects. Research persists into the long-term effects of working with VDU's while manufacturers continue to work on improving screen design. Just as important from the ergonomic point-of-view are seating, surrounding lighting and other workplace considerations which are discussed in Chapter 9.

Some people maintain that screens with green on black are most restful to the operator, while others suggest that black on white has the advantage of more closely resembling the final printed output and what the typist is used to. Of prime importance is that the screen presents a **steady flicker-free image**. This is influenced by the engineering of the tube, which will vary with each unit off the production line. You therefore need to look at a number of the same screens to evaluate the general quality.

Screens have a **brightness control** as every operator has a different preference for brightness level. There may also be times when it is preferable to dim the screen so that other staff in view cannot see confidential material being keyed (note, a touch typist will hardly look at the screen when first keying in a document). **Contrast control** is an additional aid but not a standard feature. The brightness and contrast control knobs need to be easily accessible, although some manufacturers still insist on having these at the back of the unit. New designs of VDU may allow the brightness and possibly contrast to be controlled from the keyboard.

Reflection from the screen surface can be tiring and a source of strain on the operator. Most screens now come with a non-reflective or anti-glare surface, but it is a feature that must be looked for, some being more effective than others and this being an area of prime concern to those working with VDUs.

Character Design

We explained that screen characters are formed by a dot matrix. The resolution of the matrix is defined as the number of horizontal and vertical dots used to form characters (in that order). A variety of matrix sizes are used by screen manufacturers. Characters should be clearly distinguishable, a sufficient size and a consistent design to help readability. An important factor is that relevant lower case characters have *true ascenders and descenders*. What this means is that characters such as "h" and "y" are able to rise and descend clearly from the main body of the character. To allow for this and to avoid confusion between characters such as "B" and "8", a dot matrix of at least 7 x 9 is required. More dense character matrices are becoming common allowing refinements in character shape. Look also at small characters such as vowels to see whether these are given a reasonable amount of space in the dot matrix. However, the *overall visual impression and ease of reading characters* for those using the equipment are the most important factors.

The *character range* on the current generation of VDU's is limited, but this situation is changing as the technology develops and the relative processing power of microchips continues to increase. Already some suppliers provide screens, albeit more expensive than normal, that can display mathematical symbols and non-Roman language characters: some will even show mathematical formulae with half-line integers, but such screens are the exception rather than the rule.

The Cursor

The cursor is a movable marker on the screen to indicate where the operator has reached in typing text. Control of movement is from the keyboard. The cursor can be moved around the screen to positions where insertions, deletions, and overtyping are to begin. It may take the form of a block, triangle or underline, so that it can be superimposed on an existing character. Sometimes it is signified by brightening the character at which it is positioned, then by a block or line if it falls on a space. It may also flash on and off to draw attention to it.

Since the operator works extensively with cursor movement it is important that it is *quickly and easily moved to all positions on the screen*. It must be *clearly visible*, even in a screen filled with text, but must not obscure any character at which it is positioned, nor prove distracting.

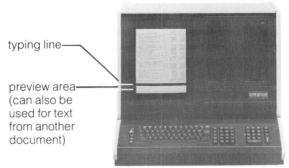

typing line

preview area (can also be used for text from another document)

Single-line cursor system – CPT 8100
Also illustrates a split-screen facility (qv)

An alternative and less common approach to a "free-moving" cursor is the *single-line cursor*. Editing or typing of each line of text can only be done at the cursor-line. Keying in text relates better to what the typist has been used to since the text moves up the screen as each new line is typed, just like a sheet of paper emerging from a typewriter. A further advantage put forward is that the typist's eyes are always focused on the same line helping to decrease eye fatigue. However, since text is continually being scrolled above the line, this may prove distracting to some operators. Locating editing points can take longer since text to be edited must be moved to the cursor-line. Since the line is part-way down the screen or even the bottom line, the amount of text that can be seen following on from an editing point is limited. It may be possible for the operator to specify which line on the screen acts as the cursor-line.

Screen Text Movement

The way in which sections of documents move to allow for text to be added as the bottom of the screen is reached, and during operations that involve jumping from one part of a document to another is important. Excessive text movement on the screen can be tiring as well as confusing in the early days of getting used to a system. Wherever possible, lines already displayed on a partially filled screen should remain still each time further material is added, and lines not being affected by an editing operation, such as an insertion or deletion should remain steady. But this is something that can only become apparent during demonstrations of different equipment.

Screen Manoeuverability

Operators should be able to pivot the screen vertically and horizontally to suit their personal requirements for viewing the display and for minimum reflection in different lighting conditions. If the screen and keyboard are not separated, ensure that positioning of the screen complements the keyboard for comfort concerning viewing distance and position of the operator's hands and arms.

Split Screen Working

This means the ability to display two associated documents or separate parts of the same document on the screen simultaneously. Since the trend is for full office automation systems, with management workstations currently being developed to try and relate to the way we work with paper files on an office desk, the feature is likely to be increasingly offered, but it is not yet common.

Keyboard

General Ergonomics

The alphanumeric keys are generally offered in QWERTY layout (QWERTZ in German-speaking countries, AZERTY in France and other parts of Europe). Many people do not realise that this is not the most efficient for fast typing of text. It was originally designed to prevent the type hammers from locking in the original design of typewriters. A few keyboard manufacturers are offering totally new designs. The most publicised of these is the Maltron. But it is difficult for these to become established as an acceptable alternative to what every typist has been trained on and become familiar with.

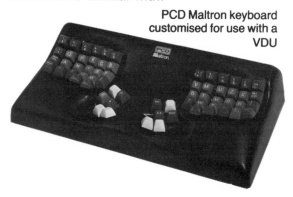

PCD Maltron keyboard customised for use with a VDU

Keyboard ergonomics is important to users of the system, and some aspects of the design are more important than others. This depends on whether a trained typist, or those familiar with computer terminal keyboards, or staff not used to a keyboard of any sort, are using the system. For typists, the preference is for key tops to be shaped similar to a standard typewriter, with a positive response to keystrokes and neither too light nor too heavy a *"touch"*. Those used to computer, terminals may be happy with less resistance to key depressions. Some people, typists and un-trained staff alike are happier if the keys also make a noise when depressed, and a few systems allow the operator to adjust the noise level of the click. Preferences may change once people become familiar with a new keyboard. The surface of key tops should be matt to reduce reflection and to prevent fingers from slipping.

Additional aids are the ability to move the keyboard around in front of the display to suit individual preferences for typing position (as well as screen viewing distance). Most keyboards now are *"detached"* in this way, and are connected to the screen only via a short cable. Some of the more recent designs have a palm rest, but the recommendation for operator comfort is for the wrists and lower arms to be horizontal. Another design feature sometimes offered is the ability to adjust the rake (the horizontal inclination) of the keyboard.

Function and Control Keys

Apart from the usual alphanumeric character set, keys are included for editing and system activities such as cursor movement, inserting, erasing, moving, formatting text in some way, or communication with the printer. These may be dedicated to the task such as "Justify", or are used in combination with others including the alphanumeric set, for example, a "Format" key plus "U" for underline mode. They are generally referred to as function or control keys. Keyboards for dedicated word processors usually have a significant number of such keys. Suppliers of microcomputer systems for extensive word processing use may also include a limited number of them. Alternatively such suppliers may offer you the option of purchasing a purpose-designed keyboard as an optional extra.

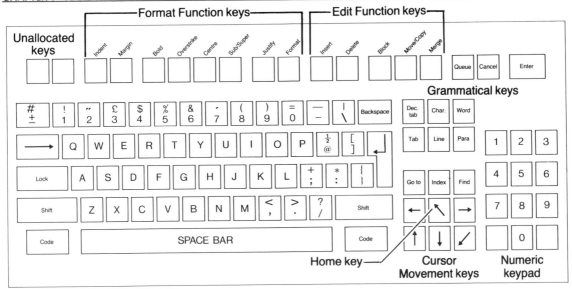

Specimen word processor keyboard lay-out

One depression of a function or control key may activate an operation, a further depression may deactivate it. In these instances it is important that the operator is given some indication as to which mode is operating – either by a message on the screen, and/or an indicator light on the key. This is also applicable to the much used shift key to indicate the locked position. However, not all keyboards offer a shift lock. Those designed for microcomputers may only have a CAPS lock which affects just the alpha keys. Yet others offer both shift and CAPS lock.

A critical set of keys are those for **_directional cursor movement_**. Since the operator uses extensive cursor movement when editing a document, it is important to be able to move the cursor to a desired position on the screen quickly and easily. It should be possible to move it right and left a character at a time, up and down a line at a time, to the start of the next line, and to the top left and bottom right-hand corners of the screen. Some of these activities may require a cursor movement key to be used in combination with another. Moving directly to the top of the current page and to the beginning and end of the document are also useful and dependent on the word processing software. With some systems the first depression of what is called the "home" key takes the cursor to the top of the current screen of text, the second depression will take it to the top of the page and

the third to the top of the document. If the system does operate in this way, an indication should be given of where the operator is in the sequence of key depressions.

A useful set of control keys are those that allow operations to be done on a word, line, sentence or paragraph at a time and referred to as **_grammatical keys_**. In conjunction with others they can be used to achieve direct cursor movement over such limits, or to delete the word, line, sentence, paragraph, or to highlight them prior to deletion, copying or movement elsewhere in the document.

The advantage of such **_dedicated keys_** is that they reduce the number of keystrokes required to carry out a particular task. They tend to make learning to use the system easier and quicker. If too many dedicated keys are offered, however, or they are badly laid out for quick access, the object of having them may be defeated. A well designed system will provide sufficient flexibility in allocation and use of keys, allowing the supplier to continue to introduce new facilities that can logically be coded with the existing keyset and quickly learned by the operator.

Whatever the range of keys offered, all should be **_clearly marked_** with the options available. This may be on the side or front face as well as the top surface. However, labels need to be short yet easily recognisable otherwise the keyboard becomes confusing to look at. Finally, it is vital that keys resulting in an irrevocable step (such as deleting a line) are not in a position where they may easily be hit in error. As a general rule it is advisable that all function and control keys are distinctly separate from the alphanumeric set.

Additional Facilities

Some keyboards offer a *repeat key* to be used in combination with alphanumerics and cursor movement, others design individual keys to automatically repeat when depressed for more than about half a second. The former has the disadvantage that the operator is required to use both hands, or at least two fingers. However, it can mean that a greater range of keys operate in repeat mode. If a repeat key is available then its position in relation to those with which it is used is important, and it should be positioned so as not to be confused with an often used key such as shift. If the second approach is offered, i.e. individual keys repeat on continuous depression, then the response to a single or continued depression should be quite distinct.

On a few systems individual keys lock to provide an extra range of characters – for example, scientific and mathematical symbols. Finally, many keyboards offer a separate *bank of numerics*, sometimes referred to as an auxiliary numeric keypad. These are a standard feature in computer terminals used for numeric data entry since sequences of numbers can be entered single-handedly. If there is likely to be extensive figure work in using your system, a numeric pad will greatly assist the operator.

In conclusion, there are many features about keyboards to look at. The only conclusive way to gain an appreciation of the design is to have those who will be using the system spend some time *trying out* the keyboard, first having allowed them time to become familiar with any unusual features.

Printer

Operations concerning printing activities as part of document processing are covered in Chapter 5. This section deals with the printers themselves. There are a number of different types of printer available, but the two most common are dot matrix and daisywheel. The latter is generally offered for dedicated word processors where it is assumed that good quality (correspondence) printout is required. Others available are also discussed.

Daisywheel Printer

The daisywheel printer was first developed by Diablo in the early 1970's and Diablo was later taken over by the Xerox Corporation. The printing element looks like a flattened daisy or spinning wheel with characters around the circumference and at the end of each petal or spoke. The daisywheel is a single-element impact printer operating on similar principles to the golf-ball typewriter. A hammer strikes the daisywheel against an inked ribbon onto the paper which is backed by the platen. The wheel rotates until the required character is in front of the hammer, the wheel stops and the hammer strikes. The daisywheel is then moved on to the next position. Some machines allow the operator to alter the hammer pressure, which can be useful on occasions to help presentation. This may be the case when a character design with a particularly light typeface is being used.

These printers are also referred to as "pet-

Daisywheel (courtesy of CBM)

al" printers. (Petal printer was the term adopted by Qume, a company later established by those originally involved with Diablo equipment). The number of characters on a wheel is usually **92, 96 or 98**. However, the word processing software may not allow the printer to access all of these. In this case, care is needed in selecting wheels to ensure that all characters required (such as £ sign, punctuation marks) are in accessible positions. In addition the sequencing may mean the position of a character on the wheel does not match the relevant key on the keyboard (and the character displayed on the screen). Some printers have been introduced that use wheels with 128 characters (Ricoh and Fujitsu models are two examples). This is achieved by providing an extra ring of characters around the circumference, sometimes referred to as dual-row daisywheels. These have the advantage that the character repertoire is much greater, which can be important when foreign language accented characters are required.

The daisywheel can be removed easily and replaced with one of another typeface or character size. **Each printer manufacturer has their own wheel design**. In the case of Diablo and Qume, wheels are interchangeable and a number of other manufacturers have designed their printers to be compatible with Diablo and Qume daisywheels. Standard character spacings or sizes are **10 and 12 pitch or proportional spacing; 15 pitch and 8 pitch** are less common options. Most printers provide at least the first three options. For those unfamiliar with the term, proportional spacing is where alphanumeric characters are given horizontal spacing proportional to their character size. A significant advantage is that some 30% – 40% more text can be accommodated on each page while also being easier to read and aesthetically more pleasing to the reader. Where documents are being printed or photocopied to any great extent, significant cost savings in reproduction are possible.

There are a **large number of daisywheel typestyles available for Qume and Diablo compatible printers** – some suppliers offer well over 100. Typestyles differ in typeface, character size and repertoire. When new printers with a unique design of daisywheel are first introduced to the market, the printer manufacturer is generally the only source of wheels. Before long, however, independent suppliers begin to offer compatible designs, so that prices become more competitive. Restrictions like these need to be considered since the cost of uniquely supplied wheels tends to be significantly more, and choice of typestyles is limited. In evaluating equipment remember that many suppliers of word processing systems use Qume and Diablo printers under their own casing and/or label.

The daisywheel most commonly used is **plastic**. A smaller selection of **metal** wheels is also available for printers designed to take them. The advantage of metal is its durability. About 5 million impressions can be obtained from a plastic wheel, 30 million from a metal one. Metal wheels also give better quality of print, but plastic quality is still very good and may be adequate for your needs. Usually the period or full-stop on plastic wheels is coated with metal to cater for extensive use of the character. The price differential between metal and plastic is not sufficient to make one significantly more economic than the other. What needs to be considered is the number of typestyles likely to be required or the desirability of experimenting with different designs. The initial investment will be considerably less with plastic wheels. An important point to watch is that some models of printer will take only metal wheels, some only plastic, some both but require a different setting within the printer. This may or may not be adjustable by the operator.

Popularly quoted speeds for daisywheel printers are **35 – 60 characters per second** (cps). It is more realistic to assume 15 cps less than the quoted maximum when relating this to typed characters on the page and for normal day-to-day operations. Some cheaper models are significantly slower, while some of the newer designs are orders of magnitude faster (80 characters per second) and this trend will continue. Many printers work bi-directionally for the majority of operations, in other words printing one line left-to-right

Proportional
spacing

then the next right-to-left. This avoids wasting time returning the carriage and wheel to the left side before it starts printing the next line. Bi-directional operation not only increases the speed of printing, it tends to mean less wear and tear caused by heavy carriage-returns.

There are some models of printer available with **dual or twin-heads**, taking two daisywheels, and designed to cater first and foremost for the scientific and mathematical document market. Although over 90 characters may seem like a reasonable number to choose from on a wheel, when special symbols are needed along with normal text, it is not really sufficient to provide the required set. With a dual-head printer, a daisywheel incorporating standard alphanumerics is used in conjunction with one having the required symbols. This approach gives more flexibility than a printer that takes one of the extended character set typestyles mentioned earlier, where the number of characters accommodated on one wheel is 128. If special symbols are a major requirement in your specification, this is an area that requires detailed attention in your selection of equipment.

Daisywheels as consumable items are discussed in more detail in Chapter 8, as are printer ribbons since each printer has its own design of ribbon cartridge. Here again it is important to consider the availability of **compatible ribbons** from independent suppliers when evaluating a printer.

Spinwriter

Another single-element device is the Spinwriter developed by NEC (Nippon Electric Company), sometimes referred to as a thimble printer since the print element looks like a thimble sitting on its base. The characters are moulded in two rows on the end of what again looks like petals which curve up from the base rather than being flat like a daisywheel. The number of characters accommodated on the thimble is **128**. These operate in essentially the same manner as the daisywheel printer and are now offered on some word processing systems. The operating speed of this printer is **35 – 55 cps**.

Golf-ball Printers

A golf-ball printer is offered as an option by some suppliers. While producing excellent quality printout, these operate typically at **15 cps** and tend to be noisier than daisywheel printers and Spinwriters. They provide cheaper options in a multi-workstation set-up. It is possible to purchase interfacing equipment which allows golf-ball typewriters produced by companies such as IBM and Sperry Remington, to be linked to certain word processors as printers. This could mean that provided the appropriate interface is available, then existing typewriters can still be put to good use, if 15 cps is an adequate speed for you.

Dot Matrix Printers

A dot matrix printer forms the characters by firing a series of small needles at the ribbon so transferring dots to the paper. They are faster and usually cheaper than the printers previously described and operate anywhere between **45 – 220 cps**. The result is however rather "dotty" in appearance which although fine for draft work and possibly internal memos and reports, is not generally good enough for business correspondence. Nonetheless, dot matrix is a well developed

Spinwriter thimble (courtesy of Willis)

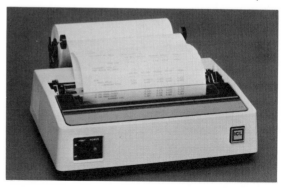

Oki Microline dot matrix printer (courtesy of ICL)

technique (for computer applications), there are a variety of suppliers who have an extensive installed base of machines, and it has proven reliability. Furthermore, the quality of output is now beginning to improve significantly in some of the newer dot matrix printers available.

The shape of the character is held electronically in the printer so that any changes in typestyle are done by printer controls. Character expansion, slanting or underline are generally used to emphasise text rather than a bold facility. Early machines used a dot matrix of 5 x 7 (horizontal by vertical) but 7 x 9 is now common; finer quality can be achieved with higher resolution matrices and overlapping dots. An example is a 40 x 18 matrix. Another way of improving quality involves slowing down the speed and making two passes over each character. Some suppliers offer the option of operating their printer at high speed for poorer quality output and at a considerably slower speed for better quality work. Bold and proportional spacing are being included as facilities on some of the newer models.

Ink-jet Printers

These were developed in the early 1970's for the computer industry. Characters are formed by spraying a very fine hair-like jet or stream of quick-drying ink onto the paper. Drops of ink are electrostatically charged as they leave a tiny nozzle. They can then be deflected with great precision to generate characters on the paper. Recent developments have employed thermal rather than electrostatic techniques. The character sets and typefaces are controlled by microprocessor software in the printer. They can be found in some shared logic systems where: high speed (90-180 cps) high volume output is required; automatic paper and, if need be, envelope handling is desirable; and where the high cost can be justified. Although ink-jet printing has been in existence for some time, it has not been until recently that fundamental design problems have been overcome and the quality improved sufficiently for it to be seriously considered for word processing applications.

Factors for Evaluation

In evaluating the printer as part of an all-inclusive system or in selecting one where

you have the choice, the aspects to consider are print quality, versatility, speed and, where appropriate, cost. Fundamental to quality and versatility is the flexibility in *horizontal and vertical spacing* and control over these (typical incremental movement offered for daisy-wheel printers is $\frac{1}{120}$ inch horizontal and $\frac{1}{48}$ inch vertical). The system is dependent on these for the following features:

- [ ] allowing variations from standard character spacing;

- [ ] sub and superscript positioning (sometimes referred to as a reverse index facility);

- [ ] right-hand justification and proportional spacing;

- [ ] printing bold;

- [ ] the facility for overprinting the previous character (useful for placing accents over characters) and for reversing a line to overprint the previous one (useful where a number of characters in a line have to be overprinted).

Some General Points

1. With small business systems where the word processing application is just one of a number of software packages used on the system, others being for example accounting or invoicing, *quality may be secondary to speed*. If not, users may have to invest in two printers – one to cope with a high volume of low quality output, the other for correspondence quality production.

2. Single-element printers (daisywheel, Spinwriter, golf-ball) produce good quality output. But they are *noisy*. However, they can be used to produce *carbon copies* – three or four can reasonably be obtained, but by the fifth characters are getting smudgy. Recent developments in daisywheel printers have led to the introduction of quieter yet faster machines. The faster the print speed, the fewer the number of good carbons likely.

3. The *width of the printer* is a factor to consider. The word processing software may allow very wide line settings but it is

no good if your printer cannot match the line width. Some will not even take A4 landscape. A few suppliers offer wide-track or wide-carriage printers – up to 28 inches. These may be necessary for statistical schedules where the master copy is often done on A3 landscape then photo-reduced, or for businesses where especially wide stationery is used.

4. Another feature to look for is a *sensing device* for end-of-ribbon so that the operator's attention is alerted with an audio signal, printing stops and continues only when a new ribbon cartridge has been loaded. It is infuriating for an operator to find that the printer has been gaily plodding on with nothing coming out on the paper because the end of the ribbon has been reached! Consider how such devices work and how easily they can be falsely activated. We know of one situation where on a particularly bright day the printer kept stopping for no visible reason. It turned out to be sunlight falling on the sensing mechanism, which was light-activated!

5. Where appropriate, *ease of changing or replacing ribbons and print elements* is important.

6. You may want to attach a *tractor-feed* to take continuous or mounted stationery, and/or a *single-sheet feeder* (otherwise known as a cut-sheet feeder or hopper-feed) for automatic feeding of single sheets of paper. Both are discussed in more detail in Chapter 8. Check that a suitable design is available to fit the printer. Check ease of fitting such devices.

7. Dot matrix and ink-jet printers theoretically can be made to reproduce any character set or design including logos and other artwork, but they are dependent on the *logic being available* to form the desired characters.

8. Some daisywheel printers will skip from the position of the last printed character to the point where the next character is to be printed, referred to as *"logic-seeking"*. This speeds up the printing and is particularly welcome when printing on a proforma or when printing a tabular document, where there are many gaps on the page.

9. Because the printer is still an electro-mechanical device, its *reliability* is low compared with the rest of the equipment in the system. Nonetheless, recent advances in printer technology have resulted in fewer mechanical parts, thus ensuring greater reliability and the need for less servicing. When something does go wrong with a microprocessor board these can be stripped out and quickly replaced. The "intelligence" in the printer is made up of a number of these boards. The replaced board is then taken back to the workshop for examination and repair.

Other developments in printer technology associated with word processing are in the area of "intelligent" printers or copiers, using laser or electrostatic printing technology to produce higher quality multiple-copy output at greater speeds and intermixing text with graphics. They effectively link word processing with document reproduction. These new technologies are still too expensive for general use. Daisywheel or Spinwriter, with dot matrix for lower quality output, are likely to be commonly used in word processing applications for some time to come.

The processor and storage

Closely linked to the processor is an internal storage facility often referred to as "the memory". Other terms used to describe this are main, primary, or working store. The second type to which we have referred a number of times, is the external storage (also referred to as external memory), which in earlier systems may have been magnetic tape or card but nowadays is provided as floppy or hard discs. External storage is used to hold the word processing software and for documents being worked on. A hard disc is a standard feature for a shared or distributed logic system. With the latter, workstations will also have floppy disc facilities.

The processor and internal memory may be physically integrated with the visual display unit (less common), be part of the unit containing the external storage medium (the disc drives), or in a shared or distributed logic system be accommodated as a completely separate unit.

The Processor

The processor is the *"nerve centre"* of the system – the central processing unit (CPU). It is what enables the equipment to carry out the various editing and formatting tasks. In all systems some of the logic (intelligence) is "hard-wired", in other words it is permanently built into the system on a microchip (sometimes referred to as firmware). In some of the earlier machines all the logic was hard-wired which meant that it could not readily be changed to introduce new functions, enhance existing ones, or add new applications, and it tended to be more limited in scope. Nowadays most of the logic is held as software on a floppy disc (referred to as the system disc) or on a hard disc and read into the internal memory in its entirety or as parts of it are needed. This is discussed in more detail in Chapter 5.

Internal Storage – The Memory

This includes areas to hold the software, areas for the processor to carry out its tasks i.e. *workspace*, and areas devoted to activities associated with the visual display as well as communication with the external storage and printer. Current developments in microchip technology are such that the size of internal memory will increase significantly over the next few years. This will lead to faster and more efficient working and the ability to do more complicated tasks, without increasing the physical size of systems or significantly increasing the cost. In fact equipment' will continue to get smaller and more compact. Note, however, that systems with good software design but relatively small internal memory, can have just as extensive facilities and speed of operation as others with several times the memory capacity.

The most popular capacity for stand-alone systems at present is *64k bytes* (equivalent to approximately 64,000 characters: 1k = 1024 a measurement used in the computer world, with a byte, another piece of computer jargon, considered equal to a character). Capacities can be considerably more or, on some of the cheaper microcomputers, less. With shared or distributed logic systems it will be considerably more.

External Storage – Floppy Discs

The floppy disc established itself as the prime external storage medium for word processors during the late 1970's. Most people are familiar by now with what they look like (a 45 rpm record or smaller). They are flexible, made of plastic and usually coated on both sides with magnetic oxide. The disc is kept in a vinyl sleeve to protect the coated surface but within this it can rotate freely with a minimum of friction. The disc is placed in the disc drive where a "head" can read or write information from and to it via a gap in the protective sleeve. The number of drives associated with a workstation, and therefore the number of discs that can be on-line at any one time, usually ranges from one to three, two being the most common.

Floppy disc in protective sleeve

Information is held on the disc in concentric tracks divided into sectors for reference purposes. Most systems now offer the facility for using a read/write sticker to protect discs from being written on (such as the system disc). This is particularly so with microcomputer systems and those that take 5¼ inch discs. There are two common sizes – *5¼ inches (sometimes referred to as mini)* and *8 inches in diameter* (3 inches is a recent innovation). What is not generally realised is the range of differences that exist between discs of the same size. These relate to:

☐ the density of storing information referred to as *single or double-density* i.e. more recording tracks are crammed on the disc;

☐ whether information is written on one or two sides and called *single or double-sided* sometimes referred to as a dual floppy or even flippy (an Americanism);

☐ whether *hard or soft sectored*, which is the means whereby the system can locate information on the disc (the former uses physical holes punched around the central hole or circumference, the latter codes one of the tracks to reference the sectors); and

□ the *way in which the system stores the information*, with some approaches being more efficient than others.

The outcome of all this is that floppy discs tend not to be compatible between different suppliers' systems. Even if the type of disc and the drive are the same, the way in which the software stores the information will differ. (Most word processing manufacturers buy in disc drives from a relatively few well-established drive manufacturers.) The only compatibility that tends to be possible is between units of the same model within a given manufacturer's range or between different word processors in the range.

The amount of information that can be stored on a floppy varies according to the factors mentioned above. A single-sided, single-density 8 inch disc will typically hold in the region of 250,000 – 300,000 characters. This may be expressed as 250k – 300k bytes. Taking an A4 page of text as anywhere between 3,000 – 4,000 characters (including spaces and line feeds) this gives 70 – 100 pages. If pages consist of simple lists the page capacity can be considerably greater. With double-sided double-density discs storage can be more than a million characters. From the users point of view the capacity is always slightly less than that quoted, due to space used by the system on parts of the disc.

The 5¼ inch floppy generally holds about a third of its 8 inch equivalent. However, with some of the newer models of drive, the capacity for double-sided double-density 5¼ inch discs can match that of their 8 inch counterparts. Mini floppy drives and discs tend to be cheaper than the 8 inch variety. Apart from generally offering less capacity on the discs, the operation of the drives lowers performance in respect of speed of accessing information on the disc. However, if your requirements are such that your work is better organised across many discs rather than wishing to accommodate more information on fewer discs, then a mini-disc system may be quite viable. Similarly, single-sided, single-density 8 inch floppies may be more suitable to your situation than higher density ones. When first introduced, double-density

and/or double-sided discs were considered less reliable but advances in technology are overcoming the initial problems.

Another factor to consider in estimating disc capacity is how much *space the software uses on the work disc* while editing is taking place. The work disc is the one used to store a new document or containing a document being edited. With some systems the previous version of a document is overwritten on the work disc as the document is being edited. With others it is not until a "save" command has been issued that the new version is permanently stored. The software may use an area of the work disc to temporarily store the new version until a "save" command is given. If this is the case, there needs to be sufficient space on the work disc for the previous and new versions. Once the "save" command has been issued by the operator, the new version will be permanently stored on the work disc and the old one deleted.

However, automatic deletion of the old version is not always the case, some software will retain the previous issue for security purposes. While offering document security, this approach effectively halves the storage capacity of the disc as all documents will have a back-up copy in the form of the previous version. The operator could chose to delete these to free space. To get a practical measure of work disc capacity, the important thing to establish is the number of pages of standard text that can reasonably be accommodated on a disc, allowing for any automatically generated back-up copies.

Despite developments in hard disc technology a new generation of floppy disc drives is emerging, with even higher storage capacity of discs and higher access speeds. But *the greater the amount of information stored, the greater the disaster* if the floppy is lost or irretrievably damaged. Adequate security procedures should eliminate such reservations. In addition, the *greater the storage and packing densities, the more accurate the disc drives* have to be in accessing information. This could have a bearing on reliability.

One of the advantages of floppy discs rather than hard discs is that external storage is theoretically limitless, discs can be carried around and used on other units of the same system type, and documents from one person's disc library can be copied to another compatible system. The disadvantage is that they are more vulnerable to contamination and processing is slower.

External Storage – Hard Discs

Hard discs resemble 33⅓ rpm records but are rigid and contained in a sealed unit or cartridge. The unit may contain a number of discs called platters. The disc with its housing may or may not be removable. The most commonly used are fixed hermetically-sealed Winchester discs. "Winchester" is used to refer to the class of sealed hard disc systems that originated at IBM in the early 1970's. It seems that the name was adopted because each of the two discs in the IBM system had a capacity of 30 megabytes. Hence 30:30 as in the renowned Winchester 30:30 rifle. (A megabyte, usually abbreviated Mb, is equal to 1 million bytes.)

The storage capacity of hard discs ranges from *5Mb – 80Mb and more* (5 million to 80 million characters). These drives and discs are more expensive than floppies but obviously hold much more information.

Until recently hard discs have been used only in multi-workstation word processing systems, but developments in the technology and relative price lowering now mean that they can reasonably be offered with stand-alone or small shared resource systems. The size of the hard discs used in computer installations is usually 14 inches in diameter while those developed for the minicomputer, microcomputer and word processing markets are 8 inches and more recently 5¼ inches or even 4 inches. Capacities of 5Mb or 10Mb are most common on stand-alone word processing systems. Larger discs with capacities of at least 20Mb and often several times this are found on large shared or distributed logic systems.

The discs are sealed in their own unit and are therefore relatively free from contamination (particularly in the case of the Winchester). They spin at greater speeds than a floppy, thus significant *improvements in performance* are achieved as finding the right position on the disc occurs that much quicker. Hard discs make the formation of small clusters of workstations more viable, with the capacity and the cost being spread across stations.

Hard disc systems should provide the option of a floppy disc drive as well. This allows documents to be copied from the hard disc to a floppy for archival storage, security, or use on another unit. Systems should also provide a facility for copying material from the disc to magnetic tape for security purposes (referred to as streaming). A small hard disc can be copied (dumped) in this way at the end of each day or week if necessary. Although hard discs do not suffer from the potential contamination problems of floppies, should something go drastically wrong with the unit, you stand to lose a great deal of material unless secure copies of work have been taken. Magnetic tape is the standard approach to dumping the entire contents of the disc – if floppies were used it would take very much longer. Provision of *dumping facilities* should be checked if you do decide to invest in a hard disc system.

An increasing number of suppliers now offer the facility for upgrading a floppy system to one with a hard disc, together with scope for adding more workstations. This could well be a viable enhancement path for the first-time buyer.

Checklist 4

CRT's for word processors and micros work on the principle of dot matrix character generation.

Screen Size:

- □ quarter, half, or full-page display – full-page is useful for complicated lay-outs;
- □ usually 80 columns wide – more can be useful for wide tables and schedules;
- □ usually 2 – 5 lines are used for a scale or ruler line and status, prompt and message lines;
- □ the control information is helpful to the operator – it should be readily monitored but not distracting.

Colour & Contrast:

- □ there are a variety of colour combinations, preferences differ;
- □ highlighting facilities are necessary but can be tiring or a source of annoyance;
- □ look for a steady flicker-free image;
- □ the brightness and contrast control knobs should be easily accessible;
- □ non-reflective properties are of prime concern.

Character Design:

- □ look for true ascenders and descenders;
- □ character range is limited but the situation is changing;
- □ the overall visual impression and ease of reading characters are important.

The Cursor:

- □ a variety of designs are used – the single-line cursor is a less common approach;
- □ it should be quickly and easily movable to all positions on the screen;

- □ it must be clearly visible even in a screen full of text.

Screen Text Movement should be minimal during operations.

Screen Manoeuverability is desirable to suit individual preferences.

Keyboard:

- □ preferences for keystroke response to touch and for feel of the keys vary;
- □ if "detached", this allows flexibility in positioning;
- □ function and control keys can be dedicated to the task or used in combination with others;
- □ directional cursor movement keys are critical;
- □ grammatical keys are useful;
- □ dedicated keys can make learning easier but not if used to excess or not readily located;
- □ clear marking and good lay-out of keys are vital to ease of use;
- □ look at the "repeat" key facility;
- □ a bank of numerics is useful for figure work;
- □ let potential operators try out and comment on the keyboards of potential suppliers.

Printer

Daisywheel Printer:

- □ usually 92, 96 or 98 characters on a wheel, with some printers now taking wheels of 128 characters;
- □ each printer has its own wheel design, but Qume and Diablo are interchangeable and work on some other printers;
- □ 10, 12 pitch and proportional spacing facilities are common, 8 pitch and 15 pitch are less so;
- □ a large number of typestyles are available

for Qume and Diablo compatible printers;

☐ plastic is cheaper but has a shorter life than metal which also gives better print quality, the printer setting for metal or plastic may be pre-set and not operator adjustable;

☐ speeds of 35 – 60 cps are common, but assume 15 cps less than the quoted maximum, some 80 cps printers are now available, many printers work bi-directionally;

☐ dual or twin-head printers are available;

☐ consider the availability of compatible daisywheels and ribbons from independent suppliers.

The Spinwriter has 128 characters on a thimble and operates at 35 – 55 cps.

The golf-ball printer operates typically at 15 cps but is a cheaper alternative.

Dot Matrix Printers are not generally regarded as correspondence quality and operate at 45 – 220 cps but quality is improving.

Ink-jet Printers are offered with some shared resource systems for high speed, high volume output where the cost is justified.

Factors for Evaluation: quality v. speed v. cost, and flexibility in horizontal and vertical spacing need to be considered.

General Points:

[1] Quality can be secondary to speed in some businesses.

[2] Single-element printers are noisy but can produce carbon copies.

[3] Consider maximum width of paper possible; wide-track printers are available.

[4] A sensing device for end-of-ribbon is useful.

[5] Ease of changing ribbons and print elements is important.

[6] Check facilities for fitting a tractor-feed or single-sheet feeder.

[7] Dot matrix and ink-jet printers are dependent on the logic available to generate the character repertoire.

[8] Logic-seeking daisywheel printers operate faster.

[9] Printer reliability is low in comparison with the rest of the system.

The Processor and Storage

The Processor: the nerve centre.

Internal storage or "the memory": used as workspace by the system, for holding the software or parts of it, and for activities concerning other equipment in the system; typically 64k bytes (characters) for stand-alone systems but considerably more is now being offered.

Floppy Discs:

☐ a range of differences lead to incompatibility between systems – 8 inch v. 5¼ inch, single v. double-sided, single v. double-density, hard v. soft sectored, the approach to storing information;

☐ watch software use of work disc space in assessing capacity of work discs;

☐ the greater the capacity, the greater the potential disaster;

☐ the greater the storage and packing densities, the greater the demands on the disc drives.

Hard Discs:

☐ a standard feature of shared and distributed logic systems;

☐ much higher capacity and performance improvements;

☐ 5 Mb to 80 Mb and more capacities;

☐ 14 inch, 8 inch or 5¼ inch;

☐ facilities for archiving to floppy and to tape are important;

☐ more expensive but possibly an enhancement path for the first-time buyer.

Software

Basic considerations

Software loading and accommodation of work
discs
Menus
Functions and the keyboard
Prompts and messages
Disc and document access
Screen display
Scrolling
Storage during editing
Document security during editing
Restricted access to discs and documents
Page or document-based
Insert and overwrite modes

Formatting

Margin setting and indentation
Right-hand justification
Hyphenation
Reformatting
Decimal tabs and statistical typing
Column work
Marking alterations for proof-correction
Pagination
Miscellaneous points on formatting

Text movement

Printing

House-keeping utilities

Checklist

Basic considerations

The design of the software (the intelligence or
logic that makes the system work) needs to be
evaluated with regard to the functions it
carries out, the efficiency of doing them, and
the dialogue that the operator has with the
system.

Software Loading and Accommodation of Work Discs

Loading the software after switching on the
equipment is often referred to as "booting"
the system. What it means is reading the
software programs stored on disc into the
internal memory for the system to carry out its
tasks. All the software or just the basic
facilities may be read in depending on the
system. A few steps may have to be gone
through in loading, such as specifying the
date and time, or a password may be needed.
With a hard disc system the software will be
held on the hard disc and loaded into the
memory every morning. With a floppy disc
system the disc holding the word processing
software, the system disc, is placed on a disc
drive and the software read into the memory.
We refer to the disc holding the documents
being input or edited as the work disc.

With floppy disc systems it is important to
understand the *requirements of the system in
accessing the software*. Remember that every
time a disc has to be read or information
stored on it, it has to occupy a disc drive.
There are a number of possibilities in accessing the software.

1. The system disc has to reside on a drive
   throughout operations. This is because
   the memory can hold only a limited
   amount of the software at a time. It will
   read certain functions or routines into its
   memory as it needs them.

2. Major sections of software can be read
   into the memory as in (1) but in discrete
   units so that the system disc can be
   removed for a time, making another disc
   drive available for a work disc. For
   example all normal editing functions may
   be read in, but when the operator comes
   to paginate a document or perhaps work
   with columns rather than text, the system
   disc may need to be reinserted and
   appropriate software read into the

memory. It may be in these instances that the system disc has to reside on the drive while such functions are being used.

3 The software can be read completely into the memory from the system disc when the machine is switched on, then the system disc removed to free the drive for a work disc.

Where the system disc can be taken out for certain operations, the stage at which this is permitted may be significant. For example, if printing a document, it may not be possible to remove the disc until printing has begun. Where a system disc has to reside on a drive throughout operations or most of the time, this means that a drive is being occupied and cannot be used for a work disc. In this case think carefully about whether you have enough drives for work discs. Consider what needs to happen when copying a document from one disc to another, if only one drive is free to accommodate the discs in question. To allow for such copying activities systems with *limited drive availability* may provide facilities for temporarily holding documents in the memory, or on some systems they may be stored temporarily on the system disc (the software parts will be protected from being overwritten by the user). The disc to be copied from can then be removed and re-placed with the one to be copied to.

Alternatively with such systems, copying from one disc to another may be a special item of software (separate from the normal word processing software) that can be read into the system and the software disc then removed. In this way a drive normally occupied by the system disc is made available for the second work disc (to be copied from or to). Bear in mind that copying documents onto a second disc could be a frequent occurrence if you decide on taking security copies of most work.

Special facilities such as sorting, checking spelling, and mathematical routines covered in the next chapter are generally supplied as separate items of software, and must be individually read into the system from the software disc when needed, perhaps even run as a separate operation outside normal word processing mode.

Some suppliers provide scope for connect-ing additional drives to individual worksta-tions to allow the flexibility of working that we have been talking about. Or it may be possible (and preferable) to choose or confi-gure a system from the outset to give this facility. To illustrate the point, consider a shared resource system with two worksta-tions sharing four drives, one of which is used to permanently accommodate the system disc. In this case there are three drives available for work discs and shared between two operators. This is more flexible than two separate stations each with two drives, but one of which has to permanently hold the system disc, so giving either operator only one drive for a work disc at any one time.

This whole area of consideration is most important to work scheduling plus conveni-ence of operation of the system, and worthy of a significant amount of attention when specifying needs and evaluating equipment. As operators become proficient and gain confidence, they are likely to tackle a variety of jobs one after the other, which may involve a number of different discs and facilities. The ability to copy a document from one disc to another while printing a document from a third disc could well be a desirable facility in a busy installation serving a number of origina-tors.

Problems of loading and unloading the software are usually not relevant to hard disc systems, since the hard disc is permanently on-line, together with all the software. Simi-larly the entire disc library is on-line, or if parts of it are archived on floppy, assuming a floppy drive is also part of the system, documents can be read in as required.

Menus

Many word processors guide the operator through major activities by consistently dis-playing lists of options on the screen. This approach is referred to as *menu-driven*. A typical menu might be:-

```
Task Selection
1 Document tasks
2 Utilities
3 Spelling Option
4 Sort Option

Type number to select task:
```

This menu could then lead to another, based on the operator's selection from the above. For example, choosing option 1 could lead to the following:-

```
Document Tasks
1 Create new document
2 Revise existing document
3 Delete document
4 Print document
5 Document index

Type number to select task:
```

Option 1 would probably lead to a menu allowing the operator to specify document format (page length, margins) and so on, until the operator is ready to enter text.

Menu-driven systems are easy to learn and can be most appropriate if equipment is to be used extensively by inexperienced staff. These systems are described by their suppliers as "user-friendly" but this approach tends to slow down the experienced, skilled operator, and ultimately can prove a source of annoyance. To avoid this, some menu-driven systems allow the menus to be by-passed. Alternatively, the operator may still be required to go through each one, but with rapid key depressions (the appropriate sequence being second-nature from constant use) the system will act without showing the intermediate screens, and significantly speed up the process of selection. Note that most systems will use lists of options i.e. menus for at least a few operations.

There are a number of points to watch for.

1. **Length and clarity of the menus** so that they are easy to follow and assimilate with options quick to specify but not at the expense of tediously increasing the number of menus in the sequence.

2. **Ease of moving around the screen** to the desired position, where the menu calls for a number of details to be specified.

3. Ease of **cancelling or correcting** an option or specification.

4. The ability to **return** to a previous menu in the sequence to make an alteration without having to cancel the operation completely and start again.

5. Ease of **withdrawing from a sequence** of menus to do something else.

A menu area frequently used by operators and employed on many systems is specifying the format of a new document. An experienced operator will appreciate being able to do so quickly with a minimum of effort.

Functions and the Keyboard
We covered keyboard design in Chapter 4 but there are a few other factors to consider about the software and keyboard use. These are itemised below. Each system has its strengths and weaknesses in these areas, some of which will prove more significant than others to your particular situation.

1. For each function or command the **number of keystrokes** in the sequence should be minimal (i.e. one or two), particularly for those that are frequently used.

2. Operations are easier and quicker to learn if a **mnemonic** approach is employed where appropriate: for example "function key" plus "L" for left margin, "function key" plus "H" for hyphenation, "function key" plus "C" for centring text.

3. Some activities require completion with an **"execute" key** – this may be labelled (Carriage) Return, Go, Send, Execute, Accept, Do, Enter. Consider carefully which operations this is used with, since it is yet another step in completing an operation. For some commands that are irrevocable, like erasing text it is preferable that such a step has to be carried out to give the operator a chance to cancel or confirm the activity.

4. Check the provision of a key for **cancelling or aborting operations**. It may be one reserved for the purpose, or a different key may be used in different situations. For example, sometimes the (Carriage) Return key is used where there is no dedicated "Cancel" or "Abort" key, or the option for cancelling may force the operator through an "ESC(ape)" route involving a further keystroke.

5. In general, **doubling-up** on the use of keys is a potential source of operator error. For example, a (Carriage) Return may be used

to forcibly end a line of text, it may also be used as an "execute" key, and in some situations to cancel a routine.

⑥ The variety of *ways of specifying text to be erased, moved or copied* is relevant to ease of operation. In particular being able to specify one character, word, line, sentence, paragraph, block of text, and even a page are all useful. Sometimes in single character deletion it is the character under the cursor that is deleted, but a "backspace-erase" command may be available. (This originates from the paper-tape typewriter days when it was useful to be able to backspace over an unwanted character and over-punch the tape to generate a code to which the tape reader did not respond.) "Backspace-erase" can be confusing to a first-time user but can be useful in immediate correction of keying errors.

⑦ In some systems certain *keys may not operate in answering prompts* or are deactivated when carrying out certain functions, all of which adds to the list of features with which the operator has to become familiar.

⑧ The limitations mentioned in points (4), (5), and (7) tend to be more characteristic of microcomputer systems running word processing software than dedicated word processors, but nonetheless should still be checked on dedicated systems.

Prompts and Messages
It is preferable for certain operations to prompt the operator with the chance to reconsider and possibly cancel an action before execution. There are other sorts of prompts, like "specify text to be deleted" or "put disc to be copied from in drive 2" and so on. Messages tell an operator that an activity has been completed, provide some form of warning, or an alert to an operational error. Examples are "name of file too long", "invalid right margin", "disc is 90% full", "permanent disc error", and "printer busy". The more interpretive these are of the problem or situation, the easier it is for the operator to take appropriate action.

Where and when the prompts and messages appear on the screen varies. It can be at the top and/or bottom. It should be possible

to notice them as they appear, but for non-critical messages they should not interfere with the current set of keystrokes. Most systems and particularly dedicated word processors will give an *audio signal* in certain instances, usually a bleep or buzz, to attract attention. The length and tone of these signals, and the frequency and extent to which they are used are relevant to "user-friendliness". They can become a source of extreme annoyance when over-used for relatively trivial situations. It may be possible to alter the noise level for operator preference.

Although not strictly a prompt, the scale and status lines are further mentioned here. In some systems this information is not always visible and has to be recalled and displayed on request. Whether a help or a hindrance will depend on what is involved in recalling them. Preferences may vary from one operator to another, but generally it is regarded as useful to have scale and status lines always present on the screen.

Disc and Document Access
A few points are discussed in this section about the way systems log or identify material on work discs and how these relate to ease of use and work organisation. The normal approach for accessing a disc is to first "log on" with a command to the appropriate drive (or in a hard disc system, a particular section of the disc), then to specify the document reference. A few floppy systems require a disc name rather than a drive number. This can be more convenient for operators since it means more to them than a drive number.

The majority of systems work within discs by document name as the reference for storing and accessing material. At least ten characters should be possible so that meaningful names can be assigned, although an experienced and well-organised operator will keep these short for ease of calling up documents. Should an operator inadvertently try to create a document with a name that already exists on the disc, it would be unusual for the system not to draw attention to the fact. However, if the duplication is between two discs brought about by copying a document from one disc to another, not all word processing software will alert you to the fact that a document already exists with the same name on the second disc. This is more likely to be the case with software run on microcomputers. In these cases the document with the same name may even be overwritten. Not an every day occurrence, but situations like this can happen and such checks are reassuring for *document security*.

A few systems work on the basis of numbers from a predefined table as the document reference, automatically allocating each new document the next number. This may even be the case for each page of a document in a page-based system (covered later in this chapter). The operator must then make sure that adequate records are kept to identify what is in each document. Whatever the approach to referencing material, adequate records should be maintained for all discs of what is held on them. It is a standard feature of word processing systems to automatically generate a *disc index* identifying all documents on a disc. The index can be viewed on the screen and printed. Additional information may include document length, date a document was last accessed, and a brief description of document contents composed by the operator.

Screen Display

Control Characters. The closer the text displayed on the screen is to the final output the better the visual impression the operator has before printing. However, systems may only allow features such as bold, sub and superscript and underline to be identified on the screen by means of the control or format characters (codes) used to define them. For example, *B* may appear immediately before and after text to be printed bold. Being able to see the real thing (for example an underline) makes it less likely for the operator to make a mistake in defining these formats, whereas it is easy to forget to put in a code to end underlining or bold formatting. Note the ability to show sub and superscripts on the screen is not common.

With some systems the space taken-up by control characters on the screen is automatically catered for by the system in displaying, for example, page boundaries. In others the operator needs to remember that the space occupied by these on the screen will disappear on printout. Subsequent text will then be displaced by the number of control characters involved. This is especially important

from the point-of-view of page boundaries, where a section of text may first appear on the screen carrying over to a subsequent page, but on printing appears on the previous page. In these systems, the operator needs to be aware of the effect of control and format characters when making decisions about possibly altering text that appears to straddle a page boundary.

Some systems provide the option of viewing the document on the screen with or without control characters. Where underlining, bold, sub and superscripts cannot be displayed, this facility does at least allow the spacing of text to be viewed as it will appear on printout. Other systems allow the operator on command to display control characters "embedded" in the system and not normally visible. However, there are a few systems where, when the full display of "embedded" control characters is switched on in this way, it is possible to physically delete them, which could lead to unnecessary operator error.

Line Endings and Margin Markers. Displaying soft or hard line endings can be helpful. A soft ending is one that will alter automatically with editing, as part of the word-wrap facility. Remember, word-wrap is a feature of all word processors and is the facility that takes care of the line ending, automatically shifting a word to the beginning of the next line if it does not fit on the current one. A hard line ending or carriage return is where word-wrap is deactivated, such as at the end of a paragraph. If subsequent editing of the paragraph alters the position of the last word, the paragraph end will be retained. With a soft line ending, any deletions from previous text will result in pulling back words from the next and subsequent lines until a hard line ending is reached. Since there are just two options, only one of them needs to be displayed to be helpful and it is usually the hard one (carriage return). Similarly, marking out margins and indentations on the screen can assist the operator.

Blocks of Text. Means of highlighting text to be copied, moved or erased should be clear but not so vibrant as to promote eye fatigue. Remember this is done by dimming the surrounding text, flashing the block of text, or using reverse video.

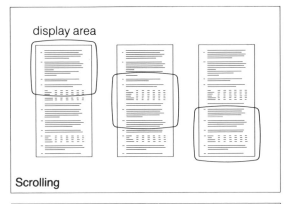

display area

Scrolling

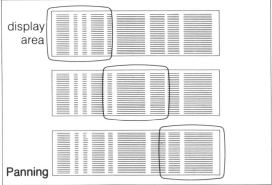

display area

Panning

Scrolling

To allow the operator to continuously view text that extends beyond the screen length, a scrolling facility is provided which rolls off text at the top of the screen while displaying subsequent lines following on from the bottom, and vice versa for moving back through text. This is not always available – with some systems the only way to view what comes before or after is to jump a screen at a'time.

The operator may be able to specify the scrolling speed – slow is convenient for an overall scan of text, going faster is desirable for moving on through a document until the required position is found. *Continuous scroll* may be specified by constant depression of the appropriate key(s), or more conveniently a key may be locked into position, or the operation started with one key depression and stopped with another. Also available may be the facility for scrolling down or up a screen or a page of text at a time, and as a result of one instruction. A two or three line overlap when scrolling in large sections helps the operator establish a reference point. It is also useful if when scrolling one or two lines at a time, the cursor is retained on the same

character rather than the same position on the screen, to provide a reference point in editing, but this is another facility that is not always available. Whatever the extent of the movement, watch how well the system copes as it may operate in a manner that can be confusing and distracting, and watch how quick the system is to react to interrupting continuous scroll.

A similar facility is often provided to cater for documents where a line width greater than the screen is required, in which case the text scrolls horizontally, otherwise called *panning*. One column disappears off to the left as another is added to the right for panning left to right and vice versa for right to left. Some systems will allow continuous panning, others do it in jumps of a block of columns. It should be possible to scroll vertically through sections of wide text, i.e. down the complete right or left-hand side, but do not take this for granted where wide-screen facilities (greater than 80 columns) are offered.

Some word processing software does not offer a panning facility at all. Where a greater number of columns can be printed than is catered for on the screen, these systems wrap the text around to the next line and use a special end-of-line marker to denote that the following text is still part of the same line. Such working is not easy for the operator and totally impractical for tabular documents, but for straightforward text, operators can get used to such limitations. This approach is more likely with microcomputers than dedicated word processors.

Storage during Editing

Where the system cannot load all the software into the internal memory, there may be a noticeable degradation in performance with some editing functions. This may produce a general slowing down in response to operator commands, or a request to "wait" may be issued until the necessary software is called into the memory. A fast typing speed may exacerbate this situation.

Parts of the internal memory are also used for the text being worked on. As the workspace becomes filled with text, the earliest part is written to disc. If the operator then wants to go back and read, revise or work on those parts already stored on (written to) disc during an editing session, the system recalls them, storing the section just worked on. All this takes time; so the advantages of having all the software loaded into memory may have to be offset against more internal memory being available as workspace for text being input or edited.

Document Security during Editing

Of prime importance is the resilience to operator error and the safeguards against a file (document) being destroyed or overwritten, or recently input text or amendments not being stored. Some systems immediately *overwrite* the old text of a document being edited. If the operator wants to retain the old version, a copy has to be made before editing begins. Other systems will automatically open a new file for the new version, leaving the previous one intact until a "save" or "end edit" command is given, at which stage the earlier version may be deleted. The crucial point with *"save"* systems is the possibility of forgetting to save the document. It is the sort of mistake that an operator tends to learn the hard way. Look for prompts by the system that will help prevent such forgetfulness. Alternatively, a power failure or system crash for some reason may occur before saving. (A "crash" means that the system becomes "frozen" and totally inoperable in the middle of an activity). With these systems it is good practice to save a long document at frequent intervals to avoid wasted effort in the likely event of this happening. And it will happen!

Where edited documents are written to a new file rather than overwriting the previous version, if the operator finishes editing part way through the document, the system should automatically copy across the remainder to the new file. The alternative is for the operator to call up the rest of the document or move to the end of it to prompt the software to copy across the remaining, unedited text. All this is time-consuming.

Some software will still retain the previous version of a document as a *back-up copy*, giving it a name that immediately identifies it as such. When a new version is created it is the previous back-up that is deleted, with the version being edited becoming the current back-up copy. For example, in the widely used word processing software package for microcomputers, Wordstar, such back-up copies are identified by .BAK attached to the document name. This means that if an operator accidentally erases a document, all is not lost, for they will be able to retrieve the previous version. Another approach is for the system to automatically store a document for a short predetermined period when the operator specifies the document to be deleted, in case it is later discovered that the text is still required.

All such approaches are helpful from a security point-of-view, but can critically affect work disc capacity. How much security of this nature is required for your organisation will depend on:

☐ the nature of the documents being held on the system;

☐ the effort involved in creating and editing documents; and

☐ the responsibilities and reliability of operators and originators.

Holding security copies on a completely different disc is even better. Document and disc security from the point-of-view of user activity are discussed in more depth in Chapter 10.

Restricted Access to Discs and Documents

If there is a need to restrict access to certain material within your organisation, a facility to put passwords on documents as well as entire discs may be required. These facilities are not always available – suppliers can argue that locking away the disc is a more practical method. If a password facility is offered, establish just what is involved in accessing discs and documents when the passwords have been forgotten or lost. It is preferable to have someone able to carry out such a task within your own organisation, rather than to send a disc to the supplier's support team for de-restricting. Not being able to restrict access to individual documents, except by putting a password on the whole disc or locking the disc away, could mean that sensitive documents have to be grouped together on a disc(s), or if documents are given "restricted access" discs to themselves much disc space is left unused.

With hard discs if there is no security facility for documents you are unlikely to be able or want to remove the disc and lock it away every night.

Page or Document-Based

Page-Based. Systems are usually described as page or document-based, the latter being most common. Document-based systems treat the document as a complete entity (provided it can be fitted on one disc). With page-based systems, the operator works in pages at a time. The maximum number of lines to a page is usually very large – for example 90. Such systems tend to work in conjunction with a *"save" command* with each page being stored on completion. Some operators find this approach tedious. Problems arise if the system allows the operator to start another page without a prompt to save the previous one. It is relatively easy for operators to forget to save a page in this way, especially if they are distracted at the critical point.

For short-life (one-off) documents some systems allow printing a page at a time such that each page can be edited and the final version printed without bothering to save any of it. The document does not then have to be deleted from the disc (since it has not officially been stored on it). It assumes the operator can take the decision as to whether the printed version is final and will not be required again. This is probably satisfactory for trivial one-off letters or where the operator is also the originator. But originators have been known to change their mind – too late.

With a page-based approach each page may have to be referenced in the disc index. Such systems are more likely to offer the facility for accessing specified line numbers than their document-based counterparts. It is not possible to scroll across page boundaries with some page-based systems. Furthermore, the way storage is organised (in discrete page blocks) can lead to editing restrictions concerning the ability to quickly and easily insert large chunks of text, or the movement of text around from one page to another.

Document-Based. With document-based systems, splitting into pages may be done as text is being input, or on a separate pagination procedure, once all text has been keyed in. If pagination is done as a separate exercise, before pagination there are no automatic reference points to jump to when editing. In these instances it is helpful if operators can put in markers as they proceed.

Once page boundaries have been created, the facility to jump backwards and forwards to a specified page within the document is usually (but not always) available, but watch how quickly the system does this. It could be that it has to automatically scroll through pages on the screen to get to the desired position, rather than jumping straight to it. Accessing a particular point in existing text that has been printed off and returned for editing, is usually easier and more reliably done by calling up the relevant page, than by any other method. The availability of such a facility and the speed with which it operates are therefore worthy of serious consideration.

Document-based systems that generate page boundaries as text is first being keyed in probably offer the greatest flexibility and ease of access, but there may be overheads to pay. These are in relation to speed of background operations such as printing, minor delays in editing activities and work disc capacity. As a user you will have to weigh up the pros and cons of the different approaches offered in relation to your applications, having tried systems out in demonstrations.

Facilities associated with setting of page lengths and subsequently altering these are discussed in the next major section of this chapter on "Formatting".

Insert and Overwrite Modes

When editing text the operator may want to replace existing characters or words or to insert additional text. An overwrite facility allows the operator to directly replace one character with another merely by typing over it (on the screen). Any remaining characters not wanted can be deleted. The text automatically closes up to fill the gap caused by the deletion.

There are two basic approaches to inserting text – in other words wherever the cursor is, any text that is typed is inserted into the document. The first approach is to instantly *"cut open"* the text at the insert point, creating space for the operator to add characters, words, lines, sentences or paragraphs. A variation is that the "cut open" action may not occur until the insert causes existing text to be pushed onto the next line. The extent of the space first created by this action varies,

```
This screen illustrates insert mode involving the "cut-open" approach.
The operator places the cursor at the insert point.  On activating insert
mode ▮

        the remaining text is dropped down to make room for the inserted
material.   Once the insert is complete the text can be reformatted with
the continuation point being pulled back automatically to the end of the
insert.
```

cursor
positioned
ready for
insert

but once used up by inserted material it is automatically extended. Sometimes as soon as inserting begins all subsequent text after the break point is temporarily stored, leaving the rest of the screen blank. However, operators can prefer to see the continuation point while keying the insertion.

Once an insert is complete, an appropriate command or even just moving the cursor past the insert point brings the continuation point back to meet the end of the insert reorganising subsequent text in the process. This action is termed *"reformatting"*. Identification of edit points in a long paragraph is easier if reformatting requires a specific command or instruction, so that the operator can move to another part of the text to do more editing before giving the command. It is easier because the line structure of the document is effectively left intact and can be related to the marked-up printed copy. It may leave the paragraph looking messy until reformatting is done, to the extent that some operators prefer to close-up after each insertion.

The second approach to inserting text involves *pushing all subsequent text along one character at a time* as the insertion is being typed. Once the end of the line is reached by the displaced text normal word-wrap takes effect. This can produce a visually disturbing ripple down the screen if a large chunk of text is being inserted, but no close-up or reformatting command is required. The system takes care of reformatting as the insertion occurs.

With many systems overwrite is the normal mode of operation and insert is activated by a command. However, there are some systems that operate *only* in insert mode. In other

Insert mode using "cut-open" approach

words it is not possible to overwrite a character. This is a secure method of working since operators must actively delete characters to erase text, they cannot accidentally overwrite something. But it does mean additional operator activity is required since all "overwrites" require insert followed (or preceded) by an erase activity. And this will probably apply also for responses to prompts such as giving document name, specifying format, and so on. Some systems operate in insert mode by default but allow operators to switch this off whenever they want to.

When the normal mode of working is "overwrite", there may be restrictions on the editing activities that can be carried out when insert mode is activated. But it is useful to be able to carry out all normal editing functions such as moving text and setting indentations while inserting text, so this point should be looked for in these systems.

Formatting

So far we have discussed the basic approach of the system to creating documents, keying in and altering text. Another major part of the software to be evaluated covers document formatting capabilities which determine how a document will appear on paper. Formatting is a standard term used in word processing when talking about activities that relate to document lay-out.

Margin Setting and Indentation

Systems may provide a default margin setting or allow the user to specify margins in a list of formatting options prior to beginning work on the document, or to change the default value. It is often desirable to be able to subsequently reset margins on document revision. To do so should be easy and require little effort. A *release facility* may be available to type within the margin – useful for section numbers or those actioned in a set of meeting minutes: if not provided, ways and means of doing so may be relatively involved such as requiring margin settings to be cancelled and reset.

However, to indent material from the main margin, systems tend to work on the basis of temporarily resetting the margin. Subsequent editing should still hold the indentations, but this is not always the case. Furthermore, some systems will allow only temporary text indentation to tab positions, sometimes referred to as *auto-tab*. This means that not only do tabs have to be set up at appropriate positions, but the facility needs to be re-activated when any of the text involved is subsequently edited.

Inserted text should follow margin settings of the text into which it is being placed, but this can cause problems if it is the first line of a paragraph where the margin has been released for a section number. Ascertaining how the software copes with such a situation should give an indication of its level of formatting sophistication. When moving text within a document of variable margins or from another document, it is likely that the setting of the section to which text is being moved will be preferred by the user and this is the common approach. There are, however, situations where a section of text with a totally different margin setting needs to be moved and its setting held. An indented quotation or a table that uses greater line width are examples. It is unusual for systems to offer the operator the option of which setting is to be adopted but to always assume one or the other. If the format of the moved text is assumed, look to see what happens to the text below the inserted material – it may be altered to match the insert, which may or may not be desirable.

Some software is sufficiently sophisticated to provide automatic paragraph numbering when required and may even sub-number according to the level of indentation of the paragraph, but such facilities are not at all common.

Right-Hand Justification

Most word processors offer this facility which gives an even right-hand margin on the printed page by padding out text with spaces to make all the lines the same length. The padding may be done by additional spaces *between words* and also by incremental spaces *between characters*. The latter is sometimes referred to as micro-justification (although this has also been used to mean other things by some suppliers). Where micro-justification does not operate, but only inter-word gaps are used, the effect can be to produce "rivers" of space through the text. The way space increments are inserted needs to be considered – the ideal is a balanced approach throughout the line. If increments are always inserted from one end till the line is filled out, the text will have excessive space at one side. Some systems show the text justified on the screen, with others justification only takes place at time of printing.

Many users on first acquiring a word processor try to impress readers of their documents by right-justifying everything. Justified text is regarded as having a somewhat formal appearance, so this needs to be taken into account in relation to the type of communication desired. For example, right-justifying standard, yet personalised letters seems to defeat the object of the apparently personal approach. The best visual effect with right-hand justification is with proportional spacing. When justification is used it is likely you will want to hyphenate words more often than normal, to avoid excessive space insertions in a line that before justification has a long gap at the end.

Hyphenation

There are two types of hyphen referred to in word processing, a soft and hard hyphen. A *soft* hyphen is one that is inserted into a word that will not fit on the end of a line, yet the hyphen will be removed or deactivated automatically if editing subsequently allows the word to fit. A *hard* hyphen is one that the operator keys in as an integral part of the word.

As mentioned in the previous section, hyphenation is particularly desirable to keep space padding to a minimum when right-hand justification is used. Some systems offer a *hyphen-help* facility in which the software searches for sections of white space at the end of lines and draws the operator's attention to those where hyphenation should be considered. This is based on a pre-set "hot zone" where, should the number of spaces at the end of a line exceed this number, the software looks at the first word on the next line, and if it thinks a suitable break can be found, the option for hyphenation is prompted.

It may be possible for the operator to set the "hot zone" or to alter a default value. With the "hyphen-help" facility a break-point is suggested for the word in question, with the option to alter it, accept it, or do without hyphenation. The recommended point is not generally based on any particularly intelligent analysis or recognition of the word, although a very few systems do have a look-up dictionary stored for suitable hyphenation points. Other systems leave hyphenation entirely to the operator to think about and specify, with no help facility.

A problem arises with decision-making for hyphenation when proportional spacing is being used, since it is rare to have a system where the screen can show proportional spacing. Except in these cases, the appearance on the screen cannot relate to the printed output, whereas fixed pitch printing (e.g. 10 and 12 pitch) has a one-to-one relationship with what is displayed (allowing for displayed control characters). Hence with proportional spacing that cannot be displayed on the screen it is difficult for the system or the operator to decide whether a hyphen is desirable.

Reformatting

When editing existing text, some systems will not reformat in terms of word-wrap, justification, or margin settings until the operator specifies this to be done. Reformatting can be tedious as well as tiresome if the operator has to watch much rippling activity on the screen while large sections of text are being done. We suggested when talking about insert mode that this approach has an arguable advantage of leaving intact text not yet edited, making it easier for the operator to follow marked-up documents. Some systems reformat in paragraphs or sections, others will do the entire document in one operation or pass (so allowing the operator to take a break or

even get on with other work), or both options may be offered. The alternative is for reformatting to take place automatically as text is edited.

Decimal Tabs and Statistical Typing

Decimal tabs are not only useful in aligning numbers with decimal points, but in aligning whole numbers or words along the right-hand edge of a column. They work as follows: the operator tabs to the decimal tab position and types the number. Each digit entered is automatically inserted immediately before the decimal point position, pushing the previously entered digit(s) one position to the left until the decimal point is keyed, after which all figures entered are inserted in the normal way i.e. one after the other towards the right-hand end of the line.

(Decimal tab position)	↓
Operator presses decimal tab key, the cursor jumps to the tab position; the operator types 2,	2
then 4,	24
followed by 6,	246
then the decimal point,	246.
followed by 1,	246.1
followed by a 2.	246.12

It would be unusual for a decimal tab facility not to be available on word processing equipment, and most will allow the operator to replace the decimal point with a comma for continental expressions, or perhaps with a wider variety of characters. If you require this, however, do confirm with the supplier that it can be done and what is involved. Check also that the decimal tab activity is not incapacitated by preceding the number with a currency sign such as £ or $, (or any other non-numeric symbol or character you wish to employ). If it is, the operator will first have to type the number then go back and put in the currency sign, or else not use the facility at all.

Column Work

Some systems now offer facilities for automatically setting columns. The operator types the longest entry in each column, then instructs the system to divide proportionately the available width of the line. Even without this level of sophistication, preparing column or table lay-outs is very much easier on a word processor than a normal typewriter. The operator, having worked out rough table widths, can quickly set headings and tab positions watching the column count on the status or ruler line, then reset any until the desired lay-out is achieved. Systems may offer the facility for moving or deleting columns, sometimes referred to as *"column-walk"*, particularly useful where a significant amount of tabular work is likely to be done. Movement may be restricted to the screen area, with any further movement required having to be done in stages by scrolling. This is a point worth checking.

One of the problems in editing columns is that when one is edited by adding or deleting a character(s), subsequent columns have to be adjusted accordingly. Hence, some word processors now allow editing within columns leaving subsequent ones intact. This may also mean that word-wrap can operate within columns. Documents such as newsletters laid out in newspaper or magazine format may benefit significantly from such a facility. The level of sophistication may be limited to word-wrap within the same column and will not work between the bottom of one column on a page and the top of another on the same page. Any significant deletions or insertions within a column therefore result in physically having to move text between columns. If a column mode of operation is likely to prove useful to you, you may also want to be able to right-hand justify each column – check that this is possible.

Marking Alterations for Proof-Correction

Since word processing means an originator theoretically need only check corrections or altered sections of the previous version of their work, some may consider the ability to mark revised text a requirement, so that these parts can quickly be identified. Changes may be highlighted by typing in red (a dual colour ribbon is required), underlining, overlining, printing in bold or overstrike, or printing a symbol or vertical line in the margin. Underlining and printing bold or overstrike may not be sufficient, as these can be confused with their normal use within the document. A facility should also be provided to identify points where a deletion has occurred.

As well as allowing the proof-corrector to quickly identify specified revisions, this marking facility has the advantage of automatically including sections that might have been mistakenly altered then retyped by the operator during editing. If a marking facility is not available or not used, originators should proof-correct text around the area of revision in case the operator has begun to alter text in the wrong place, realised the mistake, and replaced it.

Pagination

Pagination is the activity that divides the document into page lengths defined by the operator. The software may paginate the document as it is being created or as a separate operation once the document is completed. Repagination for an existing document being edited is done in the same way. The following points are important to the user.

1. How easy is it to **reset page length** throughout a document?

2. Is there a facility to **force** the start of a new page as needed despite the overall page length setting for a document? And how easily can these be removed on subsequent editing?

3. In those systems where pagination is done as a separate operation, **how long does it take** to paginate or repaginate? And can it be done in background mode i.e. the operator is allowed to carry out another task on the system while pagination is being done.

4. Does the software automatically take care of **widows** (last line of a paragraph on the top of the next page) and **orphans** (first line of a paragraph on the foot of a page), or at least draw your attention to them, and do you have a choice as to whether they are left as widows or orphans?

5. Is there a facility for marking text that, on pagination or subsequent editing, **should not be broken across a page boundary** – for example tables? This is generally achieved by placing a marker at the beginning and end of the block of text to be held intact. The software then calculates whether the block will fit on the page and if not starts it on the next page.

⑥ Does pagination automatically take account of a *resetting of line spacing* or does the operator need to change the page length? For example, the final version may be required in single spacing, 54 lines to a page but interim drafts are printed in double spacing, in which case only 30 lines can be accommodated on a page.

⑦ How easily can *headings and footings* be set up to be merged with text at time of print and what flexibility is there in specifying these? Are you limited in the number of lines or characters involved. Can you specify exactly on which pages they should be printed – you may want them only on certain pages or different headings and footings on different sets of pages? And how are these affected when individual page lengths change to cater for widows and orphans – will the space between a heading and the text remain as originally specified?

⑧ What facilities are there for *automatically numbering pages*? For example,

  □ what flexibility is there in specifying how the number is expressed and where it is typed – you may want to vary between odd and even pages;

  □ can you specify the start number – the first page may be held as a separate document as it has a different format, or the complete work may be held as a series of separate documents with continuous pagination being required across these, so that as each section (document) is printed, page numbering needs to continue on from the previous section;

  □ is it possible to have automatic decimal point page numbering for sequencing within sections or chapters – for example 6.1, 6.2,?

⑨ Some advanced systems will allow the operator to create a *"floating" footnote* which is stored separately and printed on whichever page the footnote reference exists. The system may automatically number the footnotes for you. Such facilities are not the norm but may be desirable in a publishing environment.

Miscellaneous Points on Formatting

A number of remaining points are discussed below, none of which warrants a complete section on its own, but they involve aspects that have to be considered in looking at formatting capabilities.

Spaces after full-stops. Most house-styles require two or three spaces to be typed after the end of a sentence and before the beginning of the next, unless the next starts on a new line. If subsequent editing pushes the beginning of a sentence onto a new line, the system should remove the spaces and align the sentence with the left-hand margin. It would be unusual for word processing software not to include such a feature. But not all systems will re-instate or introduce the extra spaces if the reverse occurs i.e. a sentence that started at the beginning of a line subsequently gets pulled back to the previous line. If this capability is not available, manual editing will be required in these instances to insert the spaces and the need may not always be noticed by the operator.

Centring Text. Not only is it useful to be able to centre text between main margins, but to be able to do so within indented text or columns. Not all systems will do this. Even more basic – not all systems will automatically re-centre text when margins are altered; the centring has to be respecified. Centring should also take account of any control characters in the text.

Required Join. There are instances when it is mandatory not to split characters across a line even though separated by a space, for example a person's initial followed by their surname, or a date expression written in full such as "12th November". To ensure this does not happen as a result of word-wrap, either at the time of initial keying in or on subsequent editing, a character to denote a "required join" is often available and a very useful feature.

Upper/Lower Case. Being able to convert previously typed text from one case to another by pressing just one key and running the cursor over the text or specifying the change for a word, sentence, or line, is helpful in changing document headings or references within text, but is not a feature of all systems.

Expanding Coded Expressions. Being able to specify a code sometimes referred to as an infill and which gets the system to automatically print the date, time, disc/document name and version can be useful for document headers. Another type of infill is one that allows the operator to set a series of codes within a document, such as a standard letter, and to replace the codes with variable information. The operator makes a copy of the letter and jumps from one infill (coded) position to the next to key in the variables, the system automatically assuming insert mode. The ease and flexibility in setting these up is a key factor.

Batching such variable inserts for mail-shots (for example) is discussed in the next Section on "Text Movement". In a similar vein, a few systems now offer an extensive glossary facility which also involves expansion of a coded character(s). This feature is described in the next chapter.

Variable Spacing. Variations in line and character spacing within a document may be available for visual effect provided the printer can cope with these. Whether the system automatically takes care of page boundaries to account for the variations within a document or not will affect ease of use of such a feature.

Erasing of Underline. When underline is achieved by a code on the screen placed at the beginning and end of text to be underlined, it can easily be negated by deleting these codes. But for systems where the underline is displayed on the screen and generated by giving an edit command at the time of typing, a function should be available to quickly erase the underline without the need to retype the text. As with changing upper to lower case (or vice versa), this could be running the cursor over the text in a "cancel underline" mode or specifying "cancel underline" for a word, sentence, line or paragraph at a time.

Graphics. The basic facility offered is the ability to type a vertical line, so that at least boxes can be drawn for such as questionnaires and organisation charts. Being able to print a vertical is dependent on an appropriate character being available on the print element for single-element printers, or in the printer software for dot matrix and ink-jet

printers. But not all systems even offer the vertical line facility. Conversely, more advanced systems provide scope for typing graphics by drawing continuous horizontal and vertical lines on the screen. How these come out on printing is what is important, as the screen may be more versatile in this respect than the printer! Some systems will even go as far as allowing text within a box to be edited as a complete entity.

Text movement

Systems generally allow the operator to copy or move blocks of text around within a document to be merged with existing text, but it is also a requirement to be able to do so from one document to another. (Move means the text is totally removed from the first location, unlike copy where it is left intact but duplicated elsewhere). With most systems such activity within the same document can be done directly i.e. the operator marks the block, moves to the new position, and commands the block to be moved or copied to it. Where more than one document is involved, however, the operation can be more complicated. The operator may be required to first store the block in another intermediate document or temporary storage or *scratchpad memory*, sometimes referred to as a *text register*. The current document is then closed. The document to which the block has to be copied or moved is called up, and the block read in from the intermediate document or text register. Some systems will also use text registers for block move or copy within the same document.

If a scratchpad memory is available it may be possible to store more than one block at a time. Any material held in these areas is usually lost when the system is switched off. With text movement check the limitation on the amount of text that can be moved. It may be that the screen or page boundary is a restriction in marking out a block, in which case any that are larger than this need to be moved in sections.

There is an alternative approach to copying (rather than moving) material from one document to another. It is to read in a specific page(s) from the second document when at the appropriate position in the document to which material is being copied, then to delete any unwanted text from that page. However, not all systems provide the facility for calling up a specific page from another document. It should be possible to copy not just sections of text but complete documents, giving them a new name. Document copy may be part of the utilities functions which are covered at the end of this chapter.

Where standard paragraphs are used extensively, a system that provides for storing and recalling them with a code can prove fast and efficient. Bringing standard paragraphs together in this way is sometimes referred to as *"boilerplating"* or *"cutting-and-pasting"*. The alternative is to treat the paragraphs as totally separate documents and to merge these into the document being created.

The other major aspect of merging text is sometimes referred to as ***merge-printing***. We mentioned when talking about formatting, the use of infill codes to vary standard documents. Most systems now offer the facility for setting up all the infill details of each version or issue of a standard letter on a separate file called an infill document, then to have the system automatically merge these into the letter at time of printing. Some suppliers call this batch infill.

If you envisage using a merge-print facility, check the following:

1. How easy such documents are to set up.

2. What flexibility or limitations there are in number of infill positions in the letter (or other document) and in the length of the infilled material.

3. The variation possible between individual sets of infills within a batch – for example, addresses may vary in number of lines between one recipient and another.

4. Whether notes or asides can be incorporated but not printed – the infill document can later prove useful as a checklist, where it is desirable to further qualify the infill information ("for office use" so to speak).

5. Restrictions on the order in which the variable items appear on the infill document and how these must (or not) relate to the order in which they should be merged into the standard text. The same infills may be useful for a totally different document where the variable items are ordered differently.

6. What is the effect on other activities while printing? You may find that little else can be done on the system.

Such merge-print facilities can often be used in conjunction with other pieces of software to generate the infill documents. For example extracting the data from a client file according to certain criteria being fulfilled about the clients.

Printing

Systems generally operate on the basis of storing requests to print work in a print queue until the printer is ready to deal with them. Dedicated word processors generally allow the operator to work on another document or carry out another task in the meantime. When it is possible for the operator to carry on with other work while the printer is in operation, printing is referred to as *"background"* printing. However, some limited software will not allow any other work to be carried out while printing is taking place; and the point was just made that merge-printing may restrict other activities, even if normal printing does not. Performance of other functions during background printing requires examination, as it can significantly degrade editing activities. The preference is for background printing to always give way to foreground work (i.e. document creation or editing) for priority in use of the processor and internal memory.

A few systems will allow printing from a document while it is being worked on. This is particularly true of page-based systems where the operator can be printing one page while working on another. The norm is for a document to be closed down and stored for printing, but it may be possible as an exception to this to be able to print the page currently on the screen, although the operator may not be allowed to do anything while the page is being printed. *"Screen printing"* in this way is useful when page lay-outs are being designed. The alternative is to close down the document, print the page, open up the document, make alterations, close down, print, and so on.

It is extremely useful to be able to ***specify exactly the pages to be printed in one print job***. This situation arises when doing odd final corrections to a multi-page document. Many systems will only allow specific individual

```
                                                        &1&          <
                                                        &2&      .   <

  &3&                                                                <
  &4/0&                                                              <
  &5&                                                                <
  &6&                                                                <
  &7&                                                                <
  &8/0&                                                              <
  &9/0&                                                              <

  Dear &10&,                                                         <
                                                                     <
  Thank you for your letter of the &11& enquiring about our new model T2
  answering equipment.   I am enclosing a brochure giving details about the
  product.   We have the equipment in stock and can despatch it within &12&
  days from receipt of an order.   If you have any further queries or would  <
  like to place an order with us, then please telephone me.                  <

  Yours sincerely,                                                   <
                                                                     <
                                                                     <
  &13&                                                               <
```

Merge-print letter with infill positions coded by & &

```
  JP/ec                                                              <
  12th July 1982                                                     <
  Mr A Haggard                                                       <
  Administration Manager                                             <
  Teleprinters Ltd.                                                  <
  Parry House                                                        <
  14 Block Mews                                                      <
  London SW19 5JT                                                    <
                                                                     <
  Mr Haggard                                                         <
  14th June 1982                                                     <
  3                                                                  <
  Arthur Higgins                                                     <
  *                                                                  <
  JP/ec                                                              <
  12th July 1982                                                     <
  Mr B Anthony                                                       <
  Director                                                           <
  Bluejohn Stationers                                                <
  Binding Marsh Road                                                 <
  Wickfield                                                          <
  Kent 9BS 4ZZ                                                       <
```

Merge-print infill document with sets of variable data to be merged at the infill positions. Each set is delimited by * pages, or pages within a range or consistent sequence to be printed, for example, pages 5 to 7, or all odd page numbers; whereas, the operator might want to print pages 1, 3, 6, 8 and 11 since these are the ones with corrections on them. The only way round this without such a facility is to print each page or set of pages in turn as a separate print job.

It is important to be allowed to **interrupt or suspend** printing (the paper may be wrongly positioned, the operator may realise the wrong typestyle is loaded, paper may get scrunched up). The system should respond quickly to such an instruction. In addition the following options allow considerable flexibility in starting printing again, but unfortunately are not always available:

□ start again at the top of the same page;

□ start again at the beginning of the document;

□ continue from the interruption point;

□ abandon the job.

Since the operator may not want to break-off completely from the current task it is also important to be able to continue with normal operations while printing is suspended. An added bonus is to be able to go into the suspended document and alter something on the page being printed or any subsequent text, before printing is resumed.

It is often desirable to **mix typefaces within a document** – for example, the use of italic to emphasise words or phrases. In dot matrix and ink-jet printers this is dependent on the range of typefounts stored in the printer. In single-element printers it is done in one of two ways (unless a dual-head printer is available).

1 A **stop-code** inserted at the appropriate points stops the printer and allows the operator to change the print element. If there are lots of changes, this can be time-consuming and tedious.

2 The other approach is to use **multi-pass printing** where a code signifies to the printer not to print anything but to space over text until another code is found. Once the document is finished the printed paper is run through again with the

second print element loaded. The printer then prints the text in the gaps. It may be possible to use several different typefaces in this way with a number of passes through the document. The problem with this approach is in getting paper aligned accurately each time a new pass is started. Multi-pass printing is not a common facility.

Where the printer is dual-headed, two printing elements are available at any one time, with the printer switching from one to the other as necessary, while printing takes place.

Another useful feature is a facility for **draft printing** where no action is taken on format codes (such as for bold print) but instead these codes are printed (somewhat like a printer's galley-proof). This can save printing time and ribbon use (remember bold printing involves the character being struck several times). It is well worth doing when the content of a document going through a number of draft stages is still being scrutinised, overall visual impression being left until the final draft. On a few systems **printing in columns** may be achieved by a mechanism that winds the paper back in the printer to the top of the page for each column, but this is not a common feature.

It is more convenient for the operator if **control is from the keyboard** for starting and interrupting printing, but it is a feature worth checking. Another aspect to be considered is access to the list of documents scheduled for printing, in other words the **print queue**. The operator wants to be able to access this to check what documents are in the queue and their sequence, and to be able to alter it. At the very least a facility to interrupt the queue to print an urgent document should be featured.

Printers can usually be **shared** by a number of workstations. This is the one part of the system that is unlikely to be used for much of the time by just one operator. Given a multi-station environment, sharing the printer in this way is therefore an economic proposition. What needs to be considered is the way the system copes with documents being queued from different workstations in terms of:

□ priorities;

☐ overall control of the printer; and

☐ if controlled by one workstation, whether such control can readily be switched to another.

House-keeping utilities

A number of facilities are offered to help with disc use and organisation, referred to as housekeeping utilities. They may be held with the word processing software or offered on a separate disc. The following facilities may be included.

1 **Deletion of a Document** (this can also be part of the normal word processing software).

2 **Formatting a Disc** (occasionally referred to as initialising). This means preparing it to store documents. It can also be used to "wipe" a disc clean, therefore adequate check-points should be provided to prevent operator error in formatting the wrong disc! On a few systems the supplier insists on carrying out this activity.

3 **Free Disc Space** tells the operator how much space is still available to them on a work disc. This is useful in deciding whether to start another document on the same disc if the operator believes it is becoming full, or in deciding whether to continue with a long piece of work rather than to split it and start a new document on another disc. To cater for the latter situation, it should be possible to determine free space while still editing the document.

4 **Disc Tidy**. A utility that reorganises the documents to make more efficient use of space.

5 **Disc Index** or Directory. This displays and prints the names and descriptions of documents on a disc and perhaps also details items such as document length, version, date created and amended, all of which can be useful to the operator. Systems may hold such an index alphabetically by document name or it may be in some other order.

6 **Disc or Document Copy**. Document copy may be part of the word processing software or provided as a utility. Copying

complete discs is generally one of these house-keeping utilities.

7 **Disc Validation**. A facility to check for corruption should be done when a system crash has occurred. It should identify the documents (or even pages) that are corrupt.

8 **Valid Copy**. When a disc validation shows that a disc is corrupt, it may be possible to use another utility to copy across all uncorrupted material to a new disc.

9 **Diagnostics**. Some suppliers are now providing self-test and diagnostic routines to check out equipment. These may automatically be initiated when the system is first switched on for the day. Their purpose is to allow the operator to quote information that the engineers can interpret if a piece of equipment is malfunctioning. The engineer can then come with an appropriate spare part if necessary.

The important point about house-keeping utilities is how easily and quickly they can be run, whether other work has to be interrupted and what prompts they offer for the operator to double-check before taking an irretrievable step, such as deleting a disc or document. To those who see their operators assuming significant responsibilities in running the system, the range of utilities offered will also be of concern.

Checklist 5

Accommodation of Work Discs: Seriously consider the software's use of work disc space and availability of disc drives for work discs in a floppy disc system.

Menus: menu-driven systems are helpful for the inexperienced operator but they can become tedious unless a facility allows by-passing. Watch:

1. Length and clarity.

2. Ease of moving around the menu on the screen.

3. Ease of correcting or cancelling an option.

4. Ability to return to a previous menu in the sequence.

5. Ease of withdrawing from a sequence of menus.

Functions and the Keyboard:

1. A minimum number of keystrokes is desirable in any command sequence.

2. A mnemonic approach is easier to learn.

3. Look at the use of an "execute" key.

4. Check provision of a "cancel" or "abort" key.

5. Doubling-up on the use of keys is a potential source of operator error.

6. Ways of specifying text to be erased, moved or copied is relevant to ease of operation.

7. Keys may operate differently in answering prompts.

Prompts and Messages:

☐ the more interpretive messages are of a problem the easier it is for the operator to take appropriate action;

☐ where and when prompts and messages appear is important;

☐ the use of audio signals affects "user-friendliness".

Disc and Document Access:

☐ accessing a specific work disc is usually by specifying the drive number in a floppy disc system, but a few floppy disc systems work with disc names;

☐ document names are usually assigned by the operator to identify each piece of work but a few systems allocate document references automatically;

☐ duplication of names on the same disc should be prevented by the system as a matter of security;

☐ disc indexes are automatically generated to help the operator.

Screen Display:

☐ systems may display control characters rather than the actual format printed, and the operator may be able to display these or not by choice;

☐ displaying soft or hard line endings and marking out margins and indentations on the screen can be helpful;

☐ means of highlighting blocks of text should be clear but not vibrant.

Scrolling:

☐ scrolling a screen or page at a time may be available in addition to continuous scroll;

☐ watch that cursor movement and the extent of screen movement is not confusing or distracting;

☐ look at panning facilities.

Storage during Editing: watch the effect on performance of how the system stores text during editing and on speed of jumping back and forward through a document.

Document Security during Editing:

☐ determine resilience to operator error;

☐ systems may overwrite the previous version of a document as editing proceeds;

□ some systems will not store an edited document until a "save" command is issued;

□ some systems automatically retain the previous version as a back-up copy.

Restricted Access to Discs and Documents: password facilities may be available.

Page or Document-Based:

□ page-based systems tend to work in conjunction with a "save" command;

□ page-based systems may allow documents to be printed a page at a time without saving;

□ there may be editing restrictions with page-based systems;

□ document-based systems may require pagination as a separate operation;

□ document-based systems that do pagination as text is entered offer greater flexibility and ease of access but there may be overheads.

Insert and Overwrite Modes:

□ insert mode may be by a "cut open" approach or pushing along a character at a time;

□ if "cut open" and a reformatting command is required this can help operators to identify edit points in text;

□ the "character push" approach can cause visually disturbing ripples;

□ some systems operate only in insert mode;

□ when overwrite is the normal mode, insert mode may have editing restrictions.

Formatting

Margin Setting and Indentation:

□ ease and flexibility in changing or releasing margins is important;

□ look at how indentation is done;

□ watch the approach to following margins when moving or copying text.

Right-hand Justification: spacing can be just inter-word gaps or also inter-character gaps; a balanced approach throughout the line is desirable.

Hyphenation:

□ a soft hyphen is automatically removed or deactivated if editing subsequently allows the word to fit on a line;

□ a hard hyphen is one the operator keys as part of a word;

□ some systems offer a hyphen-help facility, but problems arise with hyphen decision-making and proportional spacing.

Reformatting: some systems will not reformat when editing until a command is given, which can be tedious unless done as a complete pass throughout the document.

Decimal Tabs and Statistical Typing: being able to specify the decimal tab character may be important to you; watch that the facility is not incapacitated by a currency or other sign preceding the figure.

Column Work: some systems offer a "column-walk" facility and it may be possible to edit within columns.

Marking Alterations for Proof-Correction: a facility may be available for marking altered text.

Pagination:

1 How easy is it to reset page-length?

2 Is there a forced new page facility?

3 How long does pagination take if done as a separate operation?

4 Treatment of widows and orphans.

5 Can text be marked so as not to be broken across a page boundary?

6 Does pagination take care of resetting line spacing when draft line spacing is being used before the final version?

7. How easily can headings and footings be set up and what flexibility is offered?

8. What facilities are there for automatically numbering pages?

9. Some systems provide "floating" footnote facilities.

Miscellaneous Points on Formatting:

□ look at the treatment of spaces after full-stops;

□ consider the treatment of centred text on resetting margins;

□ a required join facility for words is useful;

□ being able to automatically convert upper and lower case one to the other is helpful;

□ infill codes for automatically printing date, time, document name, or inserting variable information is useful;

□ the system should automatically take care of page boundaries when variable spacing is used;

□ cancelling underlining should be easy;

□ sophistication in line drawing facilities varies.

Text Movement:

□ the operator may have to use a scratchpad memory or text registers;

□ screen or page boundaries may be a restriction to the amount of text moved;

□ merge-printing is usually a facility – check ease of use, number, length and order of infills and variations possible, facilities for asides (notes), and the effect on other activities while printing.

Printing:

□ background printing is usually available – check the effect on performance;

□ screen printing may be available;

□ it is useful to be able to specify exactly the page numbers to be printed;

□ look at printing interrupt facilities;

□ consider ease of changing print elements within a document (a stop-code or multi-pass printing are the two approaches);

□ a draft printing facility may be available not acting on format codes;

□ a few systems allow printing in columns;

□ control should be from the keyboard and the operator should be able to access and manipulate the print queue;

□ printers can usually be shared by workstations.

House-keeping Utilities: facilities may include document deletion, disc formatting, free disc space, disc tidy, generation of disc indexes, disc or document copying, disc validation, valid copy and diagnostics.

Additional Facilities

Search-and-replace

Sort

Spell

Glossary

Arithmetic

Forms mode

Storing keystrokes

Other applications packages

Communication links

Compatibility

Checklist

There are a variety of facilities increasingly being offered to enhance standard word processing operation. Some, like search-and-replace, may be part of the word processing software. Others, such as sort, may have to be run as a separate activity outside word processing mode. (This varies from one system to another). One of the criteria for evaluation is whether the applications can be run in **background mode** (i.e. while the operator is carrying out other word processing tasks) and what effect this has on the **performance** of the system. The alternative is that no other activities can take place while the facility is being used, which will affect work scheduling.

The additional facilities can be included in the price of the system or word processing software, or have to be paid for as extras. In a floppy disc system the disc with the appropriate software may need to reside on a disc drive while in operation. Such facilities may require extra processing power or even a hard disc to run efficiently and this could add significantly to the cost. Some may be more attractive than others to your situation, but in general they are offered to further help originators and operators make more efficient use of their time.

Search-and-replace

Searching for a pre-defined character string is becoming a standard feature of word processing software. The maximum length of string may be anything from around 20 characters to several times this. It is a facility that can be used to quickly locate a specific point in the text of an existing document as well as for more sophisticated use. Part of the feature includes being able to specify whether the string to be searched for should be replaced by another (not necessarily of the same length). A fairly obvious use is for correcting a consistently mis-spelt word or wrongly named individual.

The facility provides a means of using shorthand where the same lengthy or difficult word or phrase appears throughout a document. The operator creates a code or abbreviation for the word, types this every time the word appears, then uses the facility to replace the code with the full expression throughout the document once typing has been completed. (Some systems provide a glossary feature specifically for this situation and this is discussed later in the chapter).

There are a number of points to watch for if search-and-replace is a significant requirement for your choice of system. Some of these sophistications are likely to be available only on the more expensive systems. In the normal office routine an operator may not need to make extensive use of search (except to quickly locate specific points in a document) or search-and-replace. However, the points listed give an indication of how limited such facilities can be.

1. How *quickly* is the search or search-and-replace carried out?

2. Can the operation take place *backwards* through the document as well as forwards. (The operator may want to change only text preceding the present position in the document). If so, is backwards operation significantly slower?

3. *Matching*. Does the search assume a space in front of the character string and after it, i.e. does it treat the string as a word or will it retrieve the string from a longer word – for example dog from dogmatic or cheque from exchequer? If spaces are not assumed, the operator will have to specify these in the search string to avoid such situations.

   Will the search find the string if it is followed or preceded in the text by a punctuation mark, and if so which marks? If not and there is a chance that the word appears before a comma, full-stop, colon, or after a bracket, then separate searches to include possible punctuation marks in the search string will have to be done. Alternatively, if a space is not assumed before and after the string, punctuation marks will not pose a problem, provided only the character string is specified (without a space on either side of it).

   Is the search affected by a soft carriage return (i.e. when a character string is spread over a line ending where word-wrap is effective)? And where justified text is shown on the screen is the search affected by the fact that extra spaces will have been inserted between words?

   Is it possible to retrieve the string irrespective of whether in upper or lower case, underlined, in bold, starting with a capital letter, or is only an exact match allowed – the word may appear in a heading or be emphasised in the text? Is it possible to specify which options are required – the operator may want to retrieve the string only when in upper case or underlined?

4. If a replacement string is identified, will it replace the string exactly as specified prior to search, or *in the format of the string replaced*. For example, the search string may be specified in lower case and the system asked to search for the same word or phrase irrespective of case, then to replace it with another but in the same case as the retrieved string. Not all systems will offer the facility for replacing instances found in upper case with the new string also in upper case.

5. Is it possible to have the system automatically repeat the search (and replace) throughout the text, referred to as *global* activity? The system will stop at each point for the operator to intervene. Is it possible to specify global search-and-replace without operator intervention and is it possible to cancel the operation in mid-stream? Can the operator specify a global search (and replace) over the entire document from anywhere in the document, without physically having to jump back to the beginning?

6. Is it possible to *store* the string so that the activity can be done on an ad hoc basis throughout a document or set of documents – for example an operator may do one search followed by a batch of editing, then look for the next occurrence, and so on?

7. Is it possible to search or search-and-replace for *more than one character string at a time*, to speed the process when a number of these operations have to be carried out?

8. In a system where reformatting is normally required after an edit will *replacement by a character string of different length require reformatting* of the paragraph involved, or will this take place automatically?

9. Can a *count* of the number of occurrences of the character string be obtained, useful in analysing text for readability?

More complicated forms of search and retrieval are also available for consistently-structured files and sometimes referred to as *list or record processing*. This involves searching through a document for sets of data fulfilling specified criteria. The retrieved sets may then be copied to another file and processed in some way (such as sorting), followed by printing or merging into another document, even to the extent of treating the data as the type of merge-print document mentioned in Chapter 5. For example, a search of a client file may be made to identify all clients in a particular geographical location and the relevant details merged into a letter announcing a promotional exercise in the area.

The addition of record processing in this way, where documents are being manipulated according to the significance of their contents begins to turn word processing systems into general management tools, rather than merely tools for more efficient production of documents. If such facilities are required, the logical matching capabilities that might be offered (and require evaluation) are:

□ less than, greater than, equal, or not equal to for figures;

□ matched, not matched for a string of characters;

□ specification of a number range;

□ satisfying a number of specified criteria linked by AND, OR and NOT.

Sort

Sort software is particularly valuable where information is held in list or tabular form, such as a telephone directory. Organising material into alphabetic or numeric sequence is a job that is often left to the typist. Being able to key in the data as it has been gathered, then getting the system to do the sort can save an inordinate amount of staff time. There are a number of features to consider.

1. Restrictions on the *form and lay-out* of entries to be sorted. It could be that these have to be well-structured, for example in columns.

2. Ability to sort in ascending and descending *order*, alphabetically, numerically and chronologically.

3. The alphabetic *sequencing* employed: for example, how are capitals, full-stops, hyphens, treated? It could be very different to the convention you normally adopt and it is unlikely that you will be able to change the sequencing arrangement of the software.

4. The extent to which different data can be sorted within *levels*. As an illustration you may wish to sort chronologically, then within date by reference number, then within this alphabetically by name.

5. Restrictions on "record" *size* (i.e. the length of each entry sorted) and "file" size (i.e. the document length).

6. The *speed* of the sort.

7. Is it possible to sort data *across* a number of documents and across a number of discs? If not and several documents are involved, perhaps held on more than one disc, these will first have to be merged together.

8. Is it possible to sort on one disc and *output* to another? You may want to retain the sorted and unsorted versions on different discs as part of your disc organisation, or one disc may not be big enough to hold both versions.

Spell

A facility to check spelling of words within documents is increasingly being offered and is of benefit for checking literals and transpositions e.g "teh" for "the", "mece" for "mice" as well as genuine mispelling ("untill" for "until"). The spelling routine looks at every word within the document and matches it against a dictionary held on disc. Usually the complete sequence of characters is compared, but the procedure may involve checks on suffixes and prefixes. The system will then highlight words not found in its dictionary and allow the operator to accept or replace them. Some limited spell facilities will only list out on the screen or printer, the words that cannot be matched, giving the unrecognised word together with its page and line position.

Conversely, a few advanced systems will go as far as providing a possible alternative selected from the dictionary. If correct, all the operator need do is press a key and automatically the mis-spelt word will be replaced by the correct one. Words recommended are alphabetically close to the mis-spelt one in the dictionary. Finding a correct alternative is more likely to occur, therefore, if the mistake is near the end of the word rather than the beginning. For example, with the word "displaced", if the mis-spelling is "displaiced", the chances of being presented with the correct spelling are high. If the mis-spelling is "desplaced", the nearest words could be "despised", "despond", or others beginning with "desp".

A spell facility cannot be used in place of proof-correction, since it will not detect words missed out or mistakes involving words that do exist in the dictionary but that are typed in error.

There are a number of points to look at.

1. The *size* of the standard dictionary (about 40,000 – 50,000 words is reasonable).

2. The *language* source of the words e.g. American versus English spellings.

3. The *method* by which words are checked and how prefixes and suffixes are treated: a word such as "disspell" may be allowed if prefixes are checked separately from the rest of the word!

4. In systems that highlight errors on the screen, on correction of a mistake by the operator, is the *correction then automatically checked*?

5. Treatment of *capital letters*.

6. The option for *adding words* from your own special vocabulary and how easy it is to do this.

7. Whether words first highlighted as possible errors but accepted by the operator as correct can *automatically be added* to the dictionary.

8. The *speed* of operation, and the effect of increasing the dictionary size (if such an option is available).

Glossary

A glossary facility entails holding a list of standard abbreviations or codes that are typed instead of the full word or phrase, then the system automatically replaces these with the full text. Points to watch for are:

1. *Speed* of operation – particularly if the replacement takes place at time of keying the code rather than on completion of the document; response to the current set of keystrokes by the operator should not be significantly hampered.

2. Limitation on the *size* of the glossary.

3. Ease of *adding terms* to the glossary.

Unless such a feature is likely to be used extensively, a global search-and-replace facility may be adequate. As mentioned earlier, operators can decide on their own abbreviations at the start of the document and automatically replace them with the full word or phrase on completion. However, the character strings will not be stored for future use in this case unlike with a glossary facility.

Arithmetic

Many systems now offer basic arithmetic functions covering addition, subtraction, perhaps multiplication, division, and calculating percentages. These can be used on rows and columns of figures and sometimes on figures in text, when the originator has not already provided a result or for double-checking calculations. Extensive use may be made of such a facility in preparing budget statements, proposals, invoices, price-lists. Where a significant amount of originator time needs to be saved in complex calculations, more sophisticated facilities may be required in the form of other applications software packages that can be interfaced with the word processing software. If the type of simple arithmetic functions mentioned above are likely to prove useful and are all that is required, then check the following points.

1. *Ease of use* – the operator may have to specify by row and column numbers, or by running the cursor over relevant figures. What sort of language is used in specifying arithmetic functions?

2. Restrictions, if any, on working across screen or page *boundaries*.

3. Provision of *temporary storage areas* for

holding intermediate results. These are sometimes referred to as memory cells or registers.

④ Facilities for *skipping* certain figures within a row or column as not all figures may be relevant to the total.

⑤ Flexibility in specifying number of *decimal places*.

⑥ The ability to introduce *constants* into calculations. For example, the operator may wish to add a column of figures, then to divide by the number of figures in the column (the constant) to give the average.

⑦ Flexibility in how figures used in calculations and presented in results are *written*. In particular, are commas in figures allowed, will they automatically be placed in the result if over a thousand, how are negative numbers specified (with a "−", bracketed), and how is zero displayed ("0", "−", blank)?

⑧ The facility for carrying out calculations outside a table, sometimes called *non-tabular maths*, is useful for calculations or formulae in the middle of text.

Forms mode

Systems may allow the mask or overlay of a form to be held, with form headings protected from operator intervention or printing. The operator is allowed to type only the variable data in the appropriate unprotected positions, generally moving from one field to the next by a carriage return or tab. The data can then be printed on the preprinted form, with each item falling on the correct line or in the correct box. On completion of one form, the operator calls up another mask on the screen and proceeds with the next set of data.

Another approach to this is the "Ask Variables" facility. It may be possible to set up a series of prompts displayed one after the other on the screen and to which the operator responds with the relevant details. Another part of the software provides the facility for specifying where the responses are to be printed on the form using codes that relate to the prompts. The "Ask Variables" approach can make setting up a form and subsequent completion of the data a relatively easy task.

There are a number of important points to consider with forms mode.

Forms mode screen partially completed. The dimmed text is "protected".
The cursor is positioned ready to enter "Price"

1. How *easy* is it to set up a mask or form overlay?

2. How easy is it to get *alignment* right in printing out the data on the preprinted form?

3. How easy is it for the operator to *move around the form* on the screen from one variable field to another, or must every variable field be keyed through whether relevant or not?

4. What calculations or validation *checks*, if any, can be built into form completion? For example, it may be useful to check that a field has only alpha characters in it, or that a value is within certain limits, or to get the system to calculate one field based on the values within two others, or to store and print text in upper case even though entered in lower.

5. Is there a facility for *manipulating* the stored data in some way other than just straight printing? So often information held on a form has to be analysed or processed. You may want to use it in other word processing activities such as mailshots or compiling reports. It may be that you want to interface the forms mode data with another piece of software from the supplier.

Storing keystrokes

A number of systems offer the facility for storing a specific sequence of keystrokes that can be applied to a piece of work time and time again. These are coded into what effectively amounts to a little program, which is held like an ordinary word processing document on a disc and called into the internal memory when required.

For example a particular table may involve columns of figures where a results column is based on the multiplication of two others. Every week some of the figures in these two columns changes so that the results column also has to be changed. Once the operator has changed the first two columns, the system calls in the program and automatically recalculates the results column overwriting the previous set of figures. The approach can also be used for altering the lay-out of a page. For example, a table may consist of 4 columns of figures, each week the left-hand column is

deleted, the remaining three moved along to the left and a fourth column of new data created. The keystrokes for the column deletion and movement could be stored so that it all happens automatically on command.

Much more involved programs can be written provided a consistent sequence of keystrokes can be defined for the operation. An operator should be able to code the examples we have given without' too much trouble. More complicated applications may require additional help from the supplier's support organisation. Storing keystrokes may be a feature that does not have an immediately obvious application, but it is one that could well be desirable, once you have gained experience with a system and realise that certain documents do involve such programmable sequences of keystrokes. What needs to be evaluated is the *ease* in defining the keystrokes to be stored and the *extent of the programs* that can be written.

Other applications packages

Where a microcomputer is used with word processing software, the micro can be used to run a whole variety of software applications packages provided they have been written for a particular configuration of machine and operating system. We mentioned when talking about different types of word processing system how the operating system CP/M had become a de facto standard for the microcomputing industry. There are hundreds of packages available to run under CP/M including a number of word processing ones. They are sold by many suppliers worldwide for implementation on a vast range of computers. A number of large computer and word processing manufacturers, who normally provide their own operating systems and applications software, are now including CP/M facilities in their products.

Suppliers who package together a micro and a piece of software for the word processing market are among those who offer a variety of applications software. These tend to cover accounting and other financial application areas, particularly in relation to the running of a small business. Packages are also available from *software publishers* who are in the business of marketing and distributing software products from a wealth of sources.

At the same time, suppliers of dedicated word processors are beginning to make available a wider range of applications software.

In conclusion, anyone investing first and foremost in a micro and purchasing word processing software as just one application, is likely to have a wealth of software available to them. However, this book is about satisfying word processing needs. If there are other requirements more akin to data processing, then, as we have already indicated, further sources of help will also need to be sought.

Communication links

Increasingly, word processors are becoming equipped for communication either with other word processors, a larger computer, telex equipment, phototypesetters, optical character recognition (OCR) machines, and intelligent copiers, as the concept of the electronic office begins to take shape.

In practice, most communication still tends to be limited to other word processors of the same type or, where appropriate, to the mainframe computers of the supplier. Theoretically what is stored in digitised form on a disc can also be sent over telephone lines, cables, by satellite, and other telecommunications media to another piece of electronic equipment a few feet or several million miles away. However, this is an area requiring much expertise involving "black boxes" and pieces of software to allow the dialogue to take place, not to mention standardisation in terms of communicating languages. If you require this sort of facility it needs *detailed discussion and demonstration* with the supplier plus any other organisation whose equipment may be involved. And be prepared to devote a significant amount of time to the matter, you will find the communications expertise of some suppliers sadly lacking.

Here are explanations of a few standard terms you will come across in talking about communications (they are given in a logical order of explanation rather than alphabetically):

A *bit* is the smallest unit of information recognised by a computer with a value equal to "0" or "1". Particular patterns of 0's and 1's denote individual characters. The patterns are usually made up of eight bits, referred to as a byte.

Baud rate is a unit of data transmission speed indicating the number of times a carrier signal changes every second on a communication line. It is often, but not necessarily, equivalent to bits per second.

Asynchronous transmission means that each character being transmitted has a start/stop signal on either side of it so that the receiving equipment knows that the code for a character is about to start and when it has finished.

Bisynchronous transmission is when a block or group of characters moves along a transmission line with a start/stop signal on either side of the entire block. It is sometimes referred to as binary synchronous.

Synchronous transmission involves a constant spacing of time between units of information being transmitted, rather than using start/stop signals.

Duplex transmission means transmission can take place along a communication link in both directions at once, as opposed to *half-duplex* where transmission can take place in both directions but not at the same time.

A *modem* (modulator-demodulator) changes data fed into it to a form suitable for transmission along a particular type of communication channel. For example information coming out of a computer in the form of "bits" has to be converted for transmission along a telephone line, and likewise at the receiving end the signals will have to be converted back into "bits" of information for the receiving equipment (such as a terminal) to understand.

An *acoustic coupler* is a type of portable modem that need not be connected directly to the telephone line. The connection is made by pushing the telephone handset into two receptacles made to fit the voicepiece and earphone.

A *serial interface* is one that is used to connect equipment when bits are transmitted in serial fashion i.e. they follow each other along the wire connected to the interface. A *parallel interface* is used when bits in a byte are transmitted in parallel fashion i.e. simultaneously along 8 wires connected to the interface.

A standard communications interface on equipment is the EIA *RS232C*, which is also compatible with the CCITT *V24*. (EIA is the Electronics Industry Association and CCITT the Comite Consultatif International de Tele-graphie et Telephone.) These standards are relevant to serial interfaces and what they do is to specify electrical compatibility between pieces of equipment by defining the inter-change circuits.

A *port* is used to denote a point of entry or exit for signals into or out of a terminal or computer.

Protocols are sets of rules and conventions that allow machines to communicate intel-ligently. Some are based on agreements between organisations on an international level. Unbeknown to a telephone user, when making a call, a range of instructions and acknowledgements are transmitted between telephone exchanges as the dialling pro-ceeds, and are needed for ringing to take place, to establish connection when the tele-

phone is answered, and to disconnect. These are all part of a communications protocol.

Electronic mail means the transfer of docu-ments by electronic means over a telephone line, cable or other form of telecommunica-tion link. It is often used to refer to word processor to word processor transmission of documents.

Compatibility

By this we mean the ability to use the same external storage media on different machines. The ability or lack of it, to take floppies from one supplier's machine and run them on another involves physical characteristics of the disc, file formats, packing densities and character sets. To expand on the last point, there are different sets of codes used to represent individual characters. The EBCDIC

Checklist 6

Can these be done in background mode and if so, what is the effect on the performance of the system?

Search-and-Replace:

1. Look at the speed of the operation.

2. Can the operation take place backwards?

3. How is the character string treated with regard to spaces, punctuation marks, soft carriage returns, justified text, upper and lower case, underlining, etc.?

4. Will a replacement string assume the format of the string replaced?

5. Is global activity allowed and can it be done without operator intervention? Can a search over the entire document be started from anywhere in the document?

6. Can the string be stored for later use?

7. Can more than one character string be involved?

8. Where a system uses reformatting what happens when search-and-replace has been used?

9. Can a count of occurrences be done?

Sort:

1. Are there restrictions on the form and lay-out of entries?

2. Sorting should be possible in ascending and descending, alphabetic, numeric and chronologic order.

3. What alphabetic sequencing is used?

4. To what extent can data be sorted within levels?

5. What are the restrictions on record and file size?

6. What is the speed of the sort?

7. Can data be sorted across documents and discs?

8. Can a document on one disc be sorted and output on another?

Spell:

1. Look at the size of the dictionary.

2. Consider the language on which it is based.

3. The method by which words are checked is important.

4. Are corrections automatically checked?

5. How are capitals treated?

set is used mainly on IBM equipment and ASCII is used by most other word processing manufacturers. EBCDIC stands for Extended Binary Coded Decimal Interchange Code, and ASCII for American Standard Code for Information Interchange. In addition to using the normal alphanumeric set of characters, each manufacturer of software uses different characters or combinations of characters to code all the functions required.

In some cases there may even be problems in running the discs created on one system on another model from the same supplier.

The need for compatibility can arise because a user upgrades their system to another model, or installs more equipment of a different sort and needs to run work generated from one on the other. Or a user may want to exchange work with a different part of the organisation, a customer, supplier or collaborator. There may be scope for taking the word processing disc output as input to a subsequent process. For example, some typesetters are beginning to offer facilities for taking floppy discs and interfacing them with computerised typesetting equipment.

It is possible for programs to be written to convert from one disc format to another and some interfaces are already available. Another approach, although only to be recommended for one-time conversion and not for frequent interchange of work, is to print all documents to be converted using a suitable typeface and character size (these are limited), then the documents are run through an Optical Character Recognition (OCR) machine that can create the discs for running on the new system.

Compatibility requirements need to be *thoroughly discussed with, and if at all possible, demonstrated by your supplier*.

---

6 Can words be added to the dictionary?

7 Can words highlighted as errors but which are correct be added to the dictionary automatically?

8 Speed of operation and the effect of the dictionary size are important.

Glossary: look at speed of operation, limitations on glossary size, and ease of adding terms.

Arithmetic:

1 How easy and flexible is it to specify figures and functions?

2 Look at restrictions on working across screen or page boundaries.

3 Can intermediate results be stored?

4 Are there facilities for skipping figures?

5 What flexibility is there in specifying number of decimal places?

6 Can constants be introduced?

7 Consider the treatment of commas, negatives and zero.

8 Non-tabular maths may be available.

Forms Mode:

1 Consider ease of setting up an overlay.

2 How easy is it to get good alignment on printing?

3 How easy is it to move around the form on the screen?

4 Can calculations or validations be built in?

5 Can the stored data be manipulated for use with other wordprocessing activities or other software?

The "Ask Variables" approach is a very useful one.

Storing Keystrokes: How easy is it to define the stored keystrokes and what are the limitations on writing programs?

Other Applications Packages: anyone investing first and foremost in a microcomputer is likely to have a wealth of software available to them, particularly for the CP/M operating system.

Communication Links: if communication with other equipment is a requirement, detailed discussions and demonstrations are advised.

Compatibility: any compatibility requirements involving other equipment need to be thoroughly discussed with, and demonstrated by, the supplier.

Support

Training available

Documentation

Installation, warranty & maintenance

Enhancements

Supplier reputation

Checklist

7

Support matters cover training offered, documentation, warranty arrangements (free maintenance period), follow-on maintenance agreements, and scope for enhancement of the system. These are also an important part of any evaluation exercise.

Training available

Devising a training programme for your organisation is discussed in Chapter 11. Chapter 7 looks at what is offered in the way of formal training. Learning to use a dedicated, "user-friendly" word processing system for basic tasks can be acquired generally with about three days of good training, provided the operator does not have any fundamental difficulties in using a keyboard, or in getting used to screen work and is not afraid of using electronic equipment. If the system is not in the "user-friendly" category then grasping the basics can take several weeks. More detailed knowledge of any system's operation, use of complicated functions, full appreciation of the potential application areas, ability to run the system efficiently and to derive maximum benefit from it, all take many months more for a first-time user.

Suppliers of dedicated word processors and those who package together a word processing product may offer courses for beginners ranging from *two to five days*. Sometimes this is part of the package being sold and may even allow more than one operator to attend. Additional training can usually be arranged (at a price) either on the supplier's or customer's premises. Advanced courses or courses specifically for supervisors of the system may also be offered. Operator courses do not tend to cover the practices and procedures in running a system. These are left to the supervisor courses, which can unfortunately be lacking in the managerial and administrative aspects.

Suppliers' courses (if charged separately) are anything from £60 – £70 upwards per person per day. An alternative approach provided by some is an "on-screen", *self-teach course* where the operator is guided through a variety of exercises on a training floppy disc with accompanying documentation. Yet another approach is an audio course with tape recorder and cassette, and which again involves a training exercise disc and manual.

If you acquire a microcomputer and run a word processing package on it, then the availability from your supplier of formal training in the use of the package is more doubtful. They may instead refer you to a word processing bureau, independent training organisation, consultancy, polytechnic or local technical college for assistance in getting to grips with it. Information about independent training establishments is given in some of the sources covered in Appendix 1. If third-party training is to be used in this way, then staff are unlikely to be able to call on the training establishment for ad hoc help after the course, whereas suppliers who offer training usually make staff available at least on the telephone to help in this way.

Most companies decide to invest in formal training for one or two operators, then to rely on these people to train others within the organisation, which usually means they begin teaching others while only a few steps ahead in their own learning process. Where a number of operators are involved, there is little alternative to this approach unless you are prepared to invest heavily in formal training. But even this is not necessarily the best solution, since only so much can be learned on a formal course. Much more is gained through practical application. Selecting the right individuals to become in-house trainers is crucial to this approach.

Just as important is the attention devoted to orienting others likely to be affected in your organisation to what is involved in installing word processing equipment. Some suppliers will arrange orientation seminars, generally at a price. Such events are probably best customised to suit your particular needs. One way of approaching this is to put something together yourself and to invite the supplier to send a representative along for one or more sessions and demonstrations. Some further guidance is given in Chapter 11.

Proper training is vital to the successful implementation of a word processing system so that availability of courses and additional help when needed, warrant serious consideration in making your selection of equipment.

Documentation

The supplier may offer a variety of documentation depending on their own support organisation and how much personal assistance they are prepared to give, rather than just letting you get on with it. Most critical of all is the manual that tells you how the system works and how to use the various facilities and features. This may be the only documentation you get! Others that might be offered are a training exercise manual, a separate manual for some of the additional facilities covered in Chapter 6, a supervisor's as opposed to operator's manual (more likely for a shared logic system) and, especially useful, a quick reference card or booklet listing all the basic commands.

Indicators of good documentation are:

- □ a comprehensive, well set out table of contents – use it in evaluation of the documentation to check the structure and organisation of a manual;

- □ a detailed index (a must for any manual of the sort we have been talking about);

- □ a glossary to define special terms;

- □ summary lists and quick reference sheets of commands, error codes, and instructions, if not provided as a separate booklet;

- □ ease of identifying where a reader is in the manual – by headers giving chapter or section numbers and titles;

- □ introductions and summaries to each section to give an overview of content;

- □ a variety of examples for the reader to work through;

- □ good and plentiful illustrations of equipment, screen contents and printed documents;

- □ legibility and scanability – easily identified headings, figure captions and lists; and

- □ most important of all, how easy it is to understand!

Installation, warranty and maintenance

Installation and maintenance costs are discussed in Chapter 12 and user responsibilities in maintaining equipment are covered in Chapter 10. This section discusses the range and quality of services offered. Some suppliers now deliver equipment in modules with instructions for the customer to piece together the parts. This is likely to become more common as staff costs continue to rise and equipment prices fall. There is nothing inherently wrong with this approach provided: the equipment is well-designed for it; equipment tests are available to be carried out by the customer; immediate action is taken to replace missing parts; and a reliable telephone service is available to help iron out any difficulties. Such qualifications are best sounded out with existing customers. Most suppliers, however, send an engineer to install and test equipment, but may charge separately for this activity. If possible the person responsible for the system is well advised to watch the procedure, as they will learn aspects about the equipment that are not readily gleaned from other sources.

Details of warranty arrangements on the hardware should be scrutinised and what sort of follow-on maintenance service is offered and for how much. Warranty can be as little as a month, but is more likely to be three months (ninety days), and can be up to a year. Maintenance contracts are anywhere between twelve and twenty per cent per annum of the purchase price of the equipment. Such high percentages compared with contracts for maintenance of large mainframe computers reflect the fact that engineers' time and travel costs are not any cheaper for servicing micros or word processors. Be aware that with some warranty arrangements the customer is expected to deliver the system to the supplier's premises.

Some suppliers do not have their own engineers but sub-contract to an independent maintenance organisation. If purchasing a microcomputer, you may find that the supplier does not offer a maintenance service, but refers you to one of these contractors. In this case you will probably have several options as to the level of service: 24-hour guaranteed call-out and repair or three days to a week call-out with no guaranteed repair within that time. Alternatively, it may be possible to avoid a contract and to use a service on demand, in which case you pay heavily just for the call-out, and pay for any parts and the engineer's time by the hour. A further possibility is to take the equipment to the maintenance company's premises and to pay just for time and materials. With independent contractors the services offered for micro systems are priced for individual items, in other words the processor and drives, screen and keyboard, and the printer. However, it is sensible to have one contract covering "the system" to avoid conflict when it is not immediately clear which piece of equipment has gone wrong.

Whatever type of system you invest in, when committing to a maintenance service, seriously consider what it will mean to your organisation if and when the system becomes unavailable, and what period of "down-time" you are prepared to tolerate. It may be that you can afford to take the risk of not entering into a contract and are prepared to deliver the equipment to a maintenance contractor for repair when needed. This is more likely to be practical when you have more than one of the same system available to you. Or if there are enough systems involved, it may even be worth investing in an extra one or parts of it, such as the printer to be used as stand-by, so that you can afford to be without one for a week.

When looking at the hardware support offered from the supplier or independent contractor, there are a number of significant points to consider.

1. *Time quoted to service a call.* But it is one thing to quote a figure, another to honour it. Check the maintenance contract to see what guarantees, if any, are given about servicing calls. Asking about the size and location of the engineering force available together with the installed population of equipment serviced (number of machines) will give some idea of how geared up the organisation is to servicing calls in your area. Growth plans for dealing with an increasing customer base are also significant. Maintenance efficiency is an aspect that existing users are well placed to comment on.

2. What *fault diagnostic facilities* are available to the engineers and to the operator (to give the engineer some indication of what has gone wrong before visiting the installation)? These can greatly speed the process of repairing a fault.

3. Is it the practice to swap out microprocessor boards rather than fix

faulty ones on site? In other words the engineer arrives with a board to replace the faulty one, which is then returned to the workshops for repair. When fixed, it may be replaced in your system during another call by the engineer, or you may be left with the one the engineer fitted on first calling to repair the fault. **Board swapping** can lead to much faster repair time.

④ Servicing of some of the equipment may be carried out by a different organisation. This is particularly true of the printer. If so, ensure that arrangements and responsibilities are such that **both engineers** can be called to site when it is not obvious where the fault lies.

⑤ Is a **regular overhaul** of equipment included in the maintenance contract?

The other major support area is the software. Software usually involves some form of licence agreement and the points to consider are itemised below. In the case of a package being run on a microcomputer, the agreement is likely to be with the original supplier of the package and support is likely to be minimal, but your system supplier may be prepared to offer additional software support.

① What **service desk** facilities are available to help diagnose software problems over the telephone?

② Is a service available for retrieving work from **corrupted discs** and how quickly can these be done and returned to you?

③ Does support include **assistance** (on the end of the telephone) in using specific features or clarifying any difficulties or misunderstandings, particularly in the early days after initial training?

④ Is additional support available to **help set-up jobs** for new applications?

The next Section on "Enhancements" is also relevant to software support.

Finally the dialogue between hardware and software support functions is also key to the subject of maintenance. There will be times when it is not immediately clear whether the fault is with the hardware or the software. The organisation of support should be such that

the problem nonetheless is efficiently dealt with.

Enhancements

Suppliers tend to correct and develop their **software** as an on-going exercise. Customers should be entitled to automatically receive notification of bugs (software errors), which all software has, and subsequent issues of corrected software or software with improved features, although certain major enhancements may have to be paid for. With enhancements, good quality documentation should also be available. If the product is fairly new, a number of improvements and corrections are likely to be brought out over a fairly short period of time, so there should be some commitment to re-issue the manuals accordingly. The style of enhancements should not cause work previously set up to be incompatible or require amendment, nor should they cause significant changes to be made to the way existing features are used and have been learned by your staff.

The other area of enhancement is the **hardware** and will require investment. You may want to expand the system as part of a predetermined development plan. If so, the following may be relevant:

① To what extent can workstations be added to share the printer, and what effect does this have on performance in respect of editing and printing?

② Can further disc storage be added, either as floppy disc drives or as a hard disc?

③ Can the internal memory be expanded to improve performance?

④ To what extent can workstations be added to share the processor, internal memory and disc storage and what effect does this have on performance?

⑤ What interfaces are available for communicating to other equipment, such as another word processor?

⑥ What other equipment do they supply to interface with the word processor; for example high speed copiers, telex preparation equipment, electronic "boxes" that allow material to be recorded on magnetic media from an ordinary typewriter?

Supplier reputation

Finally, consider the background of the supplier and the history of the product. Is the product well established with a significant user population? Was it the result of a well thought-out product development plan, or was it brought out in a hurry to fill a gap in the company's product range? A number of companies have gone to the wall in this business in recent years, or have been the subject of a take-over bid or merger. Some, no doubt, still have this in store for them. If a company goes to the wall their products stand little chance of being supported by anyone else. In the case of take-over bids and mergers, a particular product may quickly be phased out with no enhancement path to those of the new proprietor.

Stability of the supplier is therefore an important issue. This requires maintaining an awareness of what is being reported in the press, finding out about the company's financial backing, as well as considering their approach to the market-place. Once convinced of the company's stability, then look to them for firm statements about product strategy and the commitment to word processing and office automation products.

Checklist 7

Training Available: proper training is vital to the successful implementation of a system:

☐ full training can take many months of hands-on experience;

☐ supplier courses tend to be 2 – 5 days, inclusive in the cost of the equipment or charged separately (£60 – £70 per person per day);

☐ audio and "on-screen" packages may be available;

☐ there are independent training organisations;

☐ suppliers may organise orientation seminars for you.

Documentation:

☐ the user manual may be the only one you get;

☐ look at pointers to good documentation – contents pages, index, glossary, quick reference sheets, headers, introductions and summaries, examples, illustrations, legibility and scanability, and how easy it is to understand.

Installation, Warranty & Maintenance:

☐ installation may be do-it-yourself or an engineer may be supplied;

☐ scrutinise warranty arrangements;

☐ maintenance may be sub-contracted by the supplier;

☐ particularly with micros, you may prefer to make arrangements with an independent contractor;

☐ hardware support – consider time quoted to service a call, fault diagnostic facilities, approach to board swapping, sharing of responsibilities between contractors, provision of a regular overhaul;

☐ software support – availability of service desk facilities, a service for corrupt discs, general assistance, support in setting-up new jobs.

Enhancements:

☐ customers should be entitled to software corrections, updates and improvements;

☐ hardware enhancement may cover additional workstations, additional disc storage, expansion of the internal memory, and communication to other equipment.

Supplier Reputation: consider the history of the product, look for financial stability, and seek firm statements about product strategy.

Consumables and Other Equipment Issues

Ancillary equipment

Tractor-feed
Single-sheet feeder
An acoustic hood

Consumables

Print elements
Printer ribbons
Floppy discs
Stationery

Checklist

There are a number of additional items associated with word processors that form part of the evaluation in selecting equipment. They include items of ancillary equipment to enhance the operation of the system, as well as consumables such as floppy discs, print elements (daisywheels, thimbles), printer ribbons, and stationery. Appendix 1 provides guidance on further sources of information about supplies of these.

Ancillary equipment

There are three items of ancillary equipment that are often required for the printer and should be considered when choosing equipment. You may not feel a need for them at the start but could well find a need in the near future. Efficient and effective use of staff time in using word processing equipment is likely to be seriously impaired if the operator has to consistently feed single sheets of paper into the printer. For efficiency it is advisable to have either a single-sheet feeder to automatically feed paper, or a tractor-feed attachment to allow continuous stationery to be used. Because both mean that printing can be left unattended, it is advisable to have a printer with a ribbon-out sensor to stop printing and attract the operator's attention. The third piece of equipment is an acoustic hood.

Tractor-feed

A tractor-feed is used to take continuous or mounted stationery (covered later in this chapter). The stationery has holes punched down the side and pins or sprockets on the feed engage in the holes to pull the paper

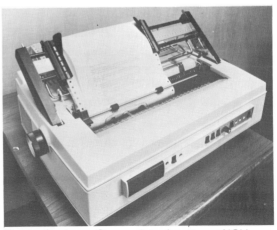

Tractor-feed on a Qume printer (courtesy of ICL)

through. It is also known as a form-feed, pin-feed or sprocket-feed.

They are available for most printers but ascertain whether your supplier has one on offer and how much it is compared to those available from an independent supplier. Costs vary from **£100 – £150**. Tractor-feeds are also useful for feeding continuous rolls of labels or for using discarded computer print-out paper for draft work. Requirements concerning the printer table when continuous or mounted stationery is used are covered in Chapter 9.

Single-sheet Feeder

A single-sheet feeder, (also known as a cut-sheet feeder or hopper-feed) is the alternative method of saving the operator having to load paper. The word processor in conjunction with the feeder will initiate the ejection of a sheet after the last line of type has been printed on a page, then load a new sheet in the correct position from a tray or stack. Single-sheet feeders have the advantage over tractor-feeds in that stationery does not have to be made up into continuous form. They are significantly more expensive (**£500 – £800**) and can be temperamental. They do offer the versatility of being able to load a range of stationery (within weight and size limitations) on demand.

Assuming there is a single-sheet feeder available to fit the printer, there are a number of critical points to consider:

- [ ] *a paper jam detector* should be incorporated to alert the operator – note the sheet-feeder will not normally stop printing when a page cannot eject properly, if this is not quickly detected incredible jams can occur;

- [ ] *reliability* – the object of having it is defeated if it needs constant attention from the operator;

- [ ] accuracy of *alignment* in positioning sheets fed in and consistency in a long print run;

- [ ] the range of *paper sizes and weights* allowed – note that use of multi-part stationery is likely to be fairly restricted, the quality of rough paper used for drafts may be limited, and accommodation of envelopes is now possible although not always available;

- [ ] the number of *feeder trays* and the means of telling the machine which paper to load – for example, letter-headed for the first page of a document, continuation for the remainder;

- [ ] *paper capacity* (at least 200 sheets is normal);

- [ ] ease of inserting paper *manually* (for odd stationery such as address labels, or if need be, envelopes) and *changing the print element or ribbon* – some machines are heavy and designed to be left in place or the sheet-feeder may have to be removed for such operations, in which case it needs to be light in weight and easy to remove and refit;

- [ ] whether the paper is ejected so that it *stacks* in a convenient way in the output tray – the norm is for the paper to drop print-side up, one page on top of the other, so that the last page of a document sits on the top;

- [ ] *warranty and maintenance* arrangements since these are expensive, precision-made items.

Check availability from the system supplier and alternative sources and the price differences.

An Acoustic Hood

The third piece of ancillary equipment, an acoustic hood, may indirectly improve staff productivity and efficiency by providing a more tolerable noise level. It will certainly improve the quality of the environment, since it fits over the printer to reduce noise. The upper noise limit for offices where mental tasks are performed is about 55 dB (decibels); above 65 dB holding a telephone conversation begins to get difficult. The noise generated by single-element printers is well above this.

The hood is made out of wood or metal, has a window in the front and top which may be opened in more than one way, and a fan to disperse the heat. Again your system supplier may have one available although they may refer you to an independent supplier. Ascertain whether there are sizes and designs available for your printer and if need be to accommodate a tractor-feed and/or single-sheet feeder. Costs are about **£300 upwards**.

 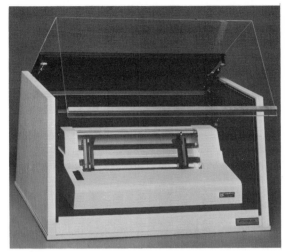

Acoustic hoods, one for a printer with a single-sheet feeder (courtesy of Powquip)

Key factors in evaluation are:

☐ **ease** of getting at the printer to change ribbons or print elements, to set-up paper with a tractor-feed, or to access the single-sheet feeder trays;

☐ level of **noise reduction** – can be anywhere between 5 dB and 20 dB;

☐ ability to **disperse the heat** from the printer and where the fan outlet is directed – if the printer is to be situated alongside the workstation, the operators will not appreciate having a gust of hot air continually directed at them;

☐ whether printing can be clearly **seen** while in progress and the resistance of the window (usually perspex) to scratches;

☐ quality of control over **lid movement** so that it can be left safely in position while the operator accesses the printer, and so that it closes in a controlled manner to avoid shocks through the hood bodywork and window.

Consumables

Throughout preceding chapters we have made reference to the consumable items associated with word processing equipment. These are of greater concern once a system has been installed but a general discussion is required here as they form a major cost element. Although an indication of item costs is given in this section, prices can vary by 20% – 30% among independent suppliers and handsome discounts may be possible for bulk purchase.

Print Elements

There are well over a hundred different typestyles (typeface, character size and repertoire) to chose from for daisywheels for Qume and Diablo compatible printers and available from a variety of consumable suppliers. The number of options of thimbles for the Spinwriter is limited by comparison, but this is a fairly recent innovation, so this situation is likely to change. Commonly used typefaces are Pica, Courier, Elite, and for sans-serif faces, Gothic and OCR-B. Standard pitches are **10 and 12 pitch**. Also useful for situations where space is tight, or as an alternative to printing on A3 and photo-reducing, is **15 pitch** which can be used on some printers, although there are very few typestyles currently offered in 15 pitch. There are a few **8 pitch** elements available, and a variety of **proportionally spaced** ones.

Some typefaces are offered in a variety of character sets to accommodate different applications. For example, a Legal or a European set is usually offered for the more common typefaces such as Pica or Courier. Special applications apart, the **character set** covered by each typestyle will vary. For example, some and not others will include a £ sign, various fractions, less common punctuation marks, and so on. These may be located at positions that can be related to the keyboard. But in some print elements they may be at positions which are labelled as something different on the keyboard, and therefore appear as a different character on the screen. Some wheels will have preferred user designs of certain characters such as the vertical line – in some, these join up neatly to form a continuous line down a page, in others they look like a string of apostrophes.

We mentioned that daisywheels are made either of *plastic or metal*, with the latter giving about six times the number of impressions before wearing out (and are correspondingly more expensive). They also give better quality print. Apart from general "wear and tear" on wheels and thimbles, a print-head may break off completely from the stem, particularly with plastic wheels. Another source of wear is caused by slight lack of synchronisation in turning the element, stopping and printing, so that the hammer strikes slightly off-centre, eventually bending the spoke and giving a warped print impression.

Qume and Diablo compatible daisywheels cost from about £6 upwards (as at mid-1982) and are more expensive if bought individually (packs of six of the same typestyle are usually the minimum). Thimbles cost slightly more, as do wheels for other makes of printer like Ricoh and Xerox, and considerably more for those where independent suppliers are not yet providing compatible elements. Metal daisywheels are *£30* upwards. Remember we said in Chapter 4 that some models of printer take only plastic wheels, some only metal, some both, but may not be adjustable by the operator and require an engineer to change the setting.

For those who require special characters in their repertoire or a completely different set of characters, organisations exist who will take an existing wheel or thimble and replace one or more of the characters, or produce a completely individual design of print element. One character change can be as much as £15 for the first change on a wheel, coming down significantly for further characters on the same element. Having your own wheel or thimble designed will require several thousand pounds, unless you can convince a manufacturer that the typestyle can ultimately be sold widely as part of their range.

Printer Ribbons

There are three types of ribbon supplied and all come in their own cartridges specifically designed for each make of printer. They are *single-strike carbon, multi-strike carbon, and cloth*. The last mentioned is by far the cheapest to use, but does not give as good quality. It is a continuous loop of nylon inked ribbon and therefore becomes fainter with use. There are some self-inking varieties which last as long as the ink supply in the cartridge but these can deteriorate if not used constantly. People generally use cloth ribbons for internal or draft work. For some, it may be possible to have cartridges re-inked by a supplier, or to use a permanent carrier and re-ink it yourself, but these approaches are not widely practised.

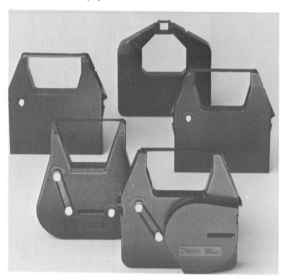

Printer ribbons (courtesy of Willis)

Carbon is recommended for better quality printing and particularly where the output is to be reproduced by quality photocopying or offset-litho printing. The single strike ribbon uses a single pass carbon film where each letter is typed on a fresh section of ribbon. It is used only where extremely high quality is required. By far the most popular is multi-strike carbon which is also a single pass ribbon and made of the same material as single strike, but the ribbon is only advanced a fraction of a character each time. On microscopic inspection some characters therefore show minor breaks, but these are not noticeable to the naked eye.

Reports on ribbon life vary considerably, because it is dependent on how much ribbon is in the cartridge. Inevitably it tends to be much shorter in practice than that quoted by suppliers. One indication is to consider 400 feet of single-strike carbon. For a 12 pitch wheel (i.e. 12 characters to the inch) the life of a single-strike ribbon would theoretically be 57,600 characters (400 x 12 x 12), about 30 reasonably full A4 pages (assuming approximately 2,000 printed characters per page); for multi-strike it would be at least four times more. However, if there is much bold used, or every time the daisywheel gets changed the operator has to wind the ribbon on a little as the exposed section became crumpled in handling, then the "life" will be significantly shorter. (The need to handle the exposed ribbon when changing a print element is a feature of some printers and not others.)

The price of different ribbon types is usually similar for a particular make of printer, perhaps a little less for cloth, a little more for single-strike. They can be bought starting at about **£4** for Qume and Diablo printers (in boxes of at least 6) and again may be more expensive for other makes of printer. In comparing costs for a particular type of ribbon the **length of ribbon in the cartridge** needs to be taken into account since it does vary from one supplier to another. The **cost of use** covers a wide range between the different types of ribbon, given the variation in useful life.

Ribbons are supplied as standard in black, but can be obtained in other colours such as grey, blue, brown, red and green. Cloth ribbons can also be obtained in two-tone, normally black with red.

Floppy Discs
In Chapter 4 we talked about different sizes and capacities of floppy discs. These again are offered by a wide range of consumable suppliers with prices starting at about **£3**. (Prices do not increase directly with storage capacity). Floppies have a limited life but some users report several years of use and some suppliers are now providing "long-life" discs based on different magnetic oxide coatings. There is no absolute figure for the life of a standard disc, but one popular quote is about two years for a disc being used constantly as a work disc. The way a disc

deteriorates is that the oxide coating starts shedding. However, useful life can be significantly reduced by poor treatment such as excessive bending, placing heavy objects on them, writing on the disc label with a sharp pen or pencil, contamination from fingers, ash, dirt, excessive exposure to sunlight, heat or humid environments. (This aspect is covered in more detail in Appendix 2). Recommended temperature ranges are 10°C – 52°C and humidity of 40% – 60% R.H. (Relative Humidity). Having said all that, it is more likely that your **floppy "consumption"** will be dictated by the way work is organised across discs and the retention period for documents.

Another factor to consider and dependent on the library of discs to be accommodated is the means of filing used. Although new floppies come in cardboard or plastic boxes that double-up as a storage medium for the floppies (within their protective jackets), it is advisable to invest in products specially designed for the job. These may be binders, wallstores, boxes, rotary units, and cabinets. There are a number of factors to think about in selecting **filing/storage items**.

☐ size of the disc library (taking into account growth rate);

☐ physical location (all next to the system, or scattered throughout an office);

☐ frequency of accessing discs or sets of discs (therefore rapid access may be required);

☐ organisation of the library (in sections, one complete sequence, the need to cater for inserts to the arrangement);

☐ security requirements (may need to be under lock and key, fireproof cabinets, separately located units for archive or security copy discs);

☐ physical environment (lots of dust, smoky atmosphere, therefore the need for greater protection).

There are only a few manufacturers of floppy discs worldwide and whatever the label on the finished product, it will have come from one of them. With such limited sourcing and the competitive nature of the market-place most suppliers have to sell within a relatively narrow price band. Anything cheaper should

Floppy disc storage units (courtesy of Willis)

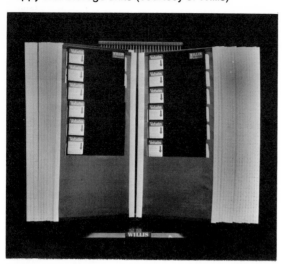

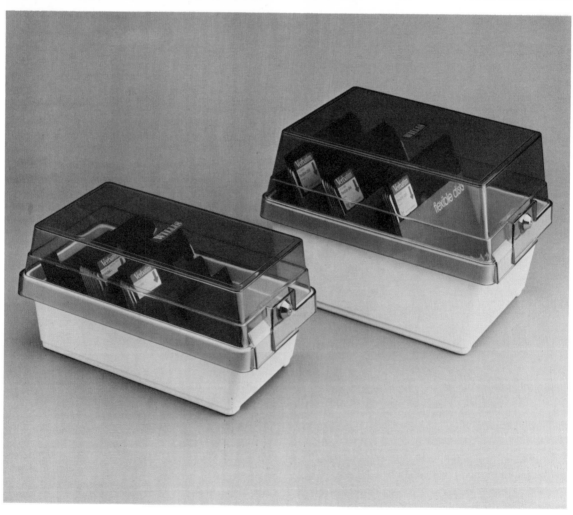

therefore be regarded with suspicion. Manufacturers of word processors may recommend a particular make of disc for their equipment. This will be based on extensive tests carried out by them. If not, or if you decide to try out a different make of floppy, it is certainly advisable to ask your system supplier for their opinion. *Poor quality media are to be avoided at all costs!*

Also relevant is the provision now of special *cleaning equipment* for floppy disc drives. Not only will atmospheric conditions affect the drives, but in the case of floppy discs contamination can be transferred to the read-write heads. Any decent maintenance contract ought to provide for regular servicing of the drives, but a number of suppliers have now introduced cleaning kits for floppy drives similar in concept to the tape cleaners for domestic audio cassette systems. The recommendation is that these are used every 2 – 4 weeks which is probably a good practice even where a maintenance contract has been signed. If you do decide to carry out such activities check with your supplier or maintenance contractor that the kit you propose to use has their approval. The cost is between £20 – £30 for a year's supply for two disc drives.

Some consumable suppliers are now making available *ring reinforcers* that can be fitted to the disc's inner hole since the inner edge can become worn and dented with constant use. This can seriously affect the alignment and rotation of the disc on the drive. You should consider investing in these (at a number of pence per disc) but check first with your word processor supplier or maintenance contractor.

Stationery

With a single-sheet feeder there is no need to organise special stationery. If a tractor-feed attachment is used, however, appropriate stationery has to be acquired either in continuous form or mounted on a carrier web. Both have holes along the right and left-hand sides to fit into sprockets on the tractor-feed allowing the paper to run continuously and unattended.

Continuous stationery means that individual sheets are joined together. This is done by perforations between one sheet and the next and between the sides of each sheet and continuous side-strips with sprocket holes in them. The side-strips are torn off after printing and the sheets separated. This is not usually satisfactory for good quality output, although the tear-off edges are hardly noticeable on good quality continuous stationery. The alternative method is to have stationery *mounted* on a special backing (web) already set up with the necessary sprocket holes. Suppliers who mount stationery in this way use different methods. It may be a hairline of gum along the complete top edge, or something resembling a stamp hinge, or a splodge of glue in two or three places at the edge. How secure this is and what traces are left once the paper is detached are aspects to evaluate.

Although there is very little extra cost involved for using plain A4 stationery in this way, if you want to have your own stationery specially printed in continuous form or mounted on a web, then significant costs are involved. A typical quote for mounting is £30 – £35 per 1,000 sheets of paper supplied. It is also important that the letter-head you supply is of good quality with regard to consistency in alignment of the pre-printed heading. An advantage of the carrier web approach is that some suppliers will take discarded web back and remount it for you. Alternatively, it proves useful for draft work.

These costs have to be weighed against the cost of investing in a single-sheet feeder, which allows standard stationery to be used within certain limits of paper weight and size. But there are situations where a single-sheet feeder can lead to investment in new stationery design. For example you may use high quality embossed letter-head or multi-part stationery that is too heavy for the feeder. Or if envelopes cannot be accommodated in the feeder, and you decide to despatch all correspondence in window envelopes, your letter-head design may not be suited to the correct positioning of addressee details and have to be redesigned. (The alternative would be to use a feeder that can also take envelopes. With a tractor-feed you can use gummed labels mounted on a web. The labels can be peeled off and stuck on the envelopes).

Checklist 8

Ancillary Equipment

A tractor-feed is used for continuous stationery and costs £100 – £150.

A single-sheet feeder is used for feeding single pages into the printer and costs £500 – £800. Check:

- [ ] reliability, accuracy of alignment, range of paper sizes and weights, paper capacity, and ease of inserting paper manually;
- [ ] availability of a paper-jam detector;
- [ ] the way the paper is stacked in the out-tray and the number of feeder-trays;
- [ ] warranty and maintenance arrangements.

An acoustic hood helps reduce printer noise. Prices are about £300 upwards. Check:

- [ ] ease of getting at the printer;
- [ ] level of noise reduction;
- [ ] ability to disperse heat and the fan position;
- [ ] whether printing can be clearly seen;
- [ ] lid movement.

Consumables

Print Elements:

- [ ] 10 and 12 pitch, proportional spacing, and occasionally 8 and 15 pitch elements are available;
- [ ] the character set of each element varies;
- [ ] daisywheels are either plastic or metal;
- [ ] there are many Diablo and Qume compatible daisywheels;
- [ ] plastic prices start at about £6, metal at £30.

Printer Ribbons:

- [ ] these are single-strike or multi-strike carbon, or cloth;
- [ ] watch differences in length of ribbon in the cartridge when comparing prices;
- [ ] the cost of use of the different types of ribbon covers a wide range;
- [ ] prices start at about £4.

Floppy Discs:

- [ ] consumption is likely to be dictated by the workload and the way work is organised rather than discs becoming worn;
- [ ] prices start at about £3;
- [ ] investment should be made in good storage units;
- [ ] there are only a few manufacturers worldwide – beware of excessively cheap discs, poor quality media are to be avoided;
- [ ] cleaning equipment for the drives can be purchased;
- [ ] ring reinforcers are available.

Stationery: the costs of having stationery mounted for use with a tractor-feed need to be weighed against the costs of a single-sheet feeder, but a single-sheet feeder can also require investment in new stationery.

PART III

People Issues and System Organisation

We begin by looking at matters to be thought about and then implemented in preparing the site for installation of a system. Many of the issues are critical to employee well-being and warrant serious attention as well as adequate investment.

Investment in word processing may be justified on the basis of increasing efficiency within the office, but installing equipment brings with it a variety of activities which, if not managed and organised properly, can generate new sources of inefficiency. Chapter 10 identifies these areas, which with due consideration will contribute significantly to getting the most out of your system.

Chapter 11 provides assistance on planning a training programme. Training can take place in a variety of ways. Selecting the right mix and making a positive investment in good training can very quickly lead to the level of returns envisaged. We look at options for familiarising and training staff, not just those using the equipment but those generating the workload or indirectly affected by the installation. And finally, attributes to look for in appointing operators and supervisors are also covered.

Planning the Installation

The location and its environment

Eyesight and other effects of VDU operation
Lighting
Heat and humidity
Noise
Space requirements
Electrical requirements
Static electricity

Lay-out

Office furniture

Workstation table
Seating
Printer table
Floppy disc drives
Additional storage facilities
Sundry items

Checklist

9

There a number of issues requiring serious attention in the early stages of planning an installation not the least of which is the accommodation of the workstation(s). Insufficient care and investment can inflict all kinds of suffering on operators – from backache, headache, and eyestrain, to psychological problems and the lowering of morale that results from physical suffering and apparent lack of concern by a manager in an employee's well-being. The outcome is reduction in quantity and quality of output.

Chapter 9 covers the three major aspects about the site. They are: location and environment; lay-out; and furniture. In some cases points of detail or final decisions can and need to be left until after the equipment has been delivered and staff have had some exposure to the system. A variety of studies covering these aspects have been carried out over recent years in conjunction with the effects of working with VDU's. For anyone who wishes, or feels the need to delve deeper, some references for further reading are given in Appendix 1. Anyone planning a large installation of equipment, where significant re-organisation of office accommodation is likely to be involved, would be well advised to consult appropriate references given in that appendix.

The location and its environment

Where is the equipment to be sited? Is the environment suitable for a word processor, but more to the point, is it suitable for the people operating the equipment? In particular, lighting, heat and humidity, noise and space requirements need to be considered.

As a general rule, 90 square feet of space is reasonable for a workstation with printer and adequate free space for operator comfort. Additional space will be required if a large disc library or bulky stationery stocks have to be accommodated.

Eyesight and Other Effects of VDU Operation

Before going on to discuss ergonomic requirements, it is appropriate to first comment on the subject of eyestrain, since this is a prime area of concern from potential operators and their employers when first introducing equipment incorporating a VDU. (In Chapter 4 we dealt with another major area of concern, radiation, and stated that research by various professional bodies has confirmed that VDU's are not harmful from emitted radiation). Eyestrain is the commonly used term for what is more explicitly described as "visual fatigue" resulting from trying to see clearly.

Research indicates that staff with previously unrealised eye defects, on transferring to VDU work from a job that is relatively undemanding visually, can become acutely aware of these. The person may be able to adjust and still tolerate the defects, alternatively fatigue may persist until the individual decides he or she needs attention. Sometimes adjustment involves the way a person sits to view the screen or document but results in an uncomfortable position, so that the symptoms then begin to relate to posture. However, it is generally agreed among the scientific and medical professions that, despite many studies, *there is no evidence yet to suggest that VDU operation has a permanent effect on the eyes or eyesight*. Nonetheless, working at a screen for prolonged periods can cause fatigue, so that rest pauses should be encouraged prior to the onset of a noticeable degree of fatigue. Pauses need not be prolonged, but must be sufficient to allow the operator to recover. Where trade unions are involved, there may be formal recommendations for frequency and length of rest pauses.

Some organisations decide to test operators for eye defects prior to taking on VDU work, as well as subsequent routine testing. Others will argue that this is unnecessary, providing that anyone suffering from eyestrain is encouraged to consult their optician, and prior to taking on the work, operators are made aware of the findings we have just discussed. People who wear spectacles for reading may need to have them corrected to provide a sufficient range of focus, given the need to look at the keyboard, screen and copy. Those who wear contact lenses may experience some problems brought about by periods of concentrated staring at the screen or source documents. This leads to a low blink rate with resultant drying of the cornea. Humidity and room temperature may need to be adjusted. These are discussed in more detail later in this section.

One issue of special importance is to ascertain whether anyone known to be an epileptic, and considered as a potential operator, suffers from photosensitive epilepsy. If so, medical advice must be sought. Longer term studies of the effects of VDU operation continue and not just in relation to eyestrain. Other areas of concern are the side-effects of certain drugs in combination with such work and a proneness of some people to skin and eye irritation as a result of build-up of electrostatic potential. (Static electricity is covered seperately later in the chapter). You should be aware of such studies while showing persistent concern for the well-being of operators.

Lighting

Positioning of the VDU needs to take into account the possibility of excessive reflection and glare. Reflection from the screen and the keyboard are usually the worst offenders.

Glare originates from windows, light fittings, reflection from the screen and other surfaces of the VDU, or other objects in the vicinity of the workstation (furniture or equipment). A non-reflective or anti-glare surface is provided on most VDU's now being sold, but some are more effective than others. Made-to-measure anti-reflective shields can also be purchased to fit on the front of screens but this may be at the expense of character brightness and resolution. No screen can be totally free from reflection, coatings and shields can only act as aids to improving the situation. Lighting is a key issue.

General positioning of the screen is critical. The facility for pivoting and tilting the VDU helps to accommodate individual preferences and changes in conditions. One of the worst situations is to have light shining directly onto the screen or into the operator's face. Lighting should be adequate for reading the material being typed or edited. Where a room gets much natural light and workstations cannot be positioned satisfactorily, installing blinds may be necessary. Care is needed in selection and use of these, otherwise they may give rise to a striped structure of reflections on the screen. Whatever the design, blinds should be easy to adjust so that operators can do so to suit the conditions. Do remember, however, that planning the location of the system for natural light conditions needs to take account of seasonal variations. Where lighting is primarily by artificial methods, unshielded fluorescent lamps are to be avoided. Glare shielding of lamps by prismatic or grid patterns is recommended.

Low levels of general illumination with individual spot lights for source documents (task lighting) is not satisfactory due to the harsh contrasts created. These can be visually uncomfortable because of the adjustments the eye has to make or even impair visual functioning. Suppliers are developing new designs of task lighting specifically for VDU work. Since individuals' preferences for lighting vary, investment in light dimmers may be worth considering as well as suitably designed task lighting that can easily be adjusted.

Heat and Humidity

Word processing systems function "in normal office environments". In terms of temperature range this is generally considered as 10°C – 35°C. Normally, this does not pose a problem but in a severe winter steps may be needed to ensure the temperature does not fall overnight to below the required minimum. However, you may find that it is the fuse in the 3-pin plug for the equipment that goes rather than anything in the system itself!

Temperature problems are far more likely to arise in relation to operator comfort. Word processing systems generate a significant amount of **heat** – the processor, disc drives, screen and printer all contribute to this.

Ventilation needs to be good or there should be some other means of adjusting the environmental temperature. If the office looks out on a busy thoroughfare, opening the windows will not be the answer. Installing the system in a spacious environment will help in dissipating heat generated. Siting also needs to take into account where the heat is blown out from equipment so that it is not directed at the operator. (It generally comes out at the back of the equipment, but can be at the front in some of the more compact designs).

In terms of humidity the "normal office environment" means 20% – 80% R.H. (Relative Humidity), but it is advisable to keep to **40% – 60% R.H.** for floppy disc care. Again, it is more likely that any humidity problems affect the operators before they do the equipment, the usual problem being that the air becomes drier than normal. While the extent is unlikely to upset most people, as mentioned earlier, contact lens wearers or those with a tendency to dry skin may suffer discomfort and it may be advisable to install a humidifier. Humidity also affects static electricity, discussed later.

Noise

All word processing systems generate noise.

The most obvious source of noise is the printer, but cooling fans on other parts of the equipment generate a constant humming. Acoustic hoods mentioned in Chapter 8 can be purchased to reduce the noise level of the printer. There is little that can be done about the hum of cooling fans. Fortunately in most machines, this is a relatively low level background noise of which operators soon become tolerant. Again, siting in spacious surroundings may help to dissipate noise, as does carpeting and even curtains. Acoustic panelling or screening may also be desirable. Switching off equipment when it is not being used for extensive periods is considerate practice.

Operators will probably need to use a telephone while working on the system and neither they nor the person at the other end of the line should have to strain to hold a conversation. If a secretary is working at a station outside a manager's office, it should be possible to hear the manager call out or buzz on a nearby telephone or intercom.

The environmental noise around the system is just as important. Operators have to concentrate on some of the more involved tasks and may find background noise from other offices or equipment intolerable at such times. The noise level for others not using the equipment but situated close-by should also be considered. Not only printer noise can be distracting but also the cooling fans, keyboard clatter and system bleeps (audio signals).

Space Requirements
We have mentioned the advantages of spacious surroundings in relation to noise and thermal environment. While word processing is still a relatively new application within an organisation, an installation is bound to attract much attention – and this means visitors. Furthermore, in situations where a number of staff are serviced, there may be a general coming and going of people to discuss their work. This is so particularly in the early days when managers and staff are learning just what the system can do, and what options are open to them in the way of document lay-out and text manipulation. The inquisitive will have to be accommodated (without disturbing those working on the system), and perhaps trainees if the system is being used extensively for operator training.

But what about the operators themselves? They will want to get in and out of seating positions to access different parts of the equipment (printer, and possibly floppy drives if not desk-top size). Furthermore, responsibilities and workflow should be designed to provide operators with the chance to assume a less static posture and to get up and move around in carrying out their daily work routine.

We mentioned earlier that where the workload leads to extensive periods of operating the system, *rest pauses* should be encouraged to prevent excessive build-up of fatigue. Short and frequent pauses tend to be more effective but there is no hard and fast recommendation. Much will depend on the nature of the workload and the individual and adequate attention to the ergonomic factors covered in this chapter are critical.

Electrical Requirements
If planning a shared logic or shared resource system laying out power supplies and com-

munication links will be a major planning exercise involving your supplier and building services staff. If installing just one or two workstations the major concern is the requirement for number and position of sockets. Check plug requirements when getting a specification of the equipment. Building regulations may mean that additional wall sockets have to be fitted. (There may be restrictions for safety regulations on the use of adaptors). Whatever the type of installation, ensure there are still spare sockets for other office equipment (desk lights, electric fan, or even the office cleaner's vacuum cleaner). And remember that electricians tend to be in short supply. This planning activity should not be left to the last minute even for a single stand-alone system!

Some offices suffer from what is referred to as a "dirty" mains supply where irregular voltage, often caused by other electrical equipment in the vicinity, can adversely affect the operation of a word processor. It may be equipment as trivial as an electric typewriter or office percolator, or more demanding items such as photocopiers and lifts. Mains conditioners can be fitted to overcome this problem. The possible need for them should be checked with your supplier's engineers before installation.

Static Electricity

The power level at which electronic circuits operate is small compared to the possible high level of static electricity that can be generated in an office. Significant static discharges can affect VDU's and if discharged into a disc drive while in operation can corrupt data. In most offices static electricity is unlikely to be as severe as this, but nonetheless should not be ignored from the point-of-view of possible staff discomfort. A number of *preventative steps* can be taken, some more extreme than others depending on the level of the problem. These are outlined below.

1. Carpets: the most common cause of static electricity, especially in centrally heated offices, is the action of people walking on the carpet. Carpets can be purchased with anti-static properties.

2. Equipment: all equipment should be properly earthed and chairs with metal

rather than plastic castors help to discharge the static.

3. Humidity: humidifiers help maintain an adequate level of moisture. In particular, moisture retained in carpets helps them to discharge static as it is formed.

4. Sprays: carpets can be sprayed with anti-static material. this may need to be done as often as once a month close to, equipment.

5. Anti-static mats: these can be purchased to provide a discharge path to a ground cord and laid out in front of the workstation.

6. Indoor plants: these can help to maintain adequate humidity levels since moisture is generated in the growing process.

Lay-out

Before settling finally on a location, some more detailed aspects about the lay-out of the equipment need to be catered for to ensure that they can be satisfied by the chosen site.

1. Operators need *frequent access to the printer* to load new stationery and pick up work even when using a tractor-feed or single-sheet feeder.

2. There should be ready and safe *access to all sockets* for switching the equipment on and off.

3. A *telephone* should be available close to the workstation for operators to take calls. It should be sufficiently close for them to carry out tests and follow instructions by their support organisation in times of serious fault situations. A receiver fitted so that it can be rested on the shoulder freeing both hands or a loudspeaker telephone are particularly helpful, as the operator may need to use both hands in such situations.

4. There will be restrictions on *cable length* between each piece of equipment. It is advisable to get hold of the exact cable specification from the supplier before planning the lay-out.

5. Maintenance engineers may have to get to the *back of equipment*.

6. If continuous or carrier stationery is to be

used there should be adequate *clearance behind the printer* for the paper being fed into and out of it, and for someone to set up the stationery and collect the output. Single-sheet feeder trays likewise should be accessible.

7 As well as generating noise, the *printer vibrates* and for this reason is best situated on a separate table. It should definitely not be placed directly on top of the floppy disc drives if these lend themselves to this. Spongy cushions can be bought to place under printers and are provided as standard by some suppliers. Absorbing the vibrations in this way also helps increase the reliability of the equipment, since one of the major sources of printer failure is loosening of internal connections.

8 *Additional work surfaces* should be provided for collating papers, or for an originator to mark-up copy or make notes. Such space may also have to accommodate the floppy disc library, daisywheel library, and ready supply of printer ribbons. Surfaces should be matt to reduce reflection.

9 If a system is to be treated as a *reference or training installation* for other departments or external organisations, then it is better to be hived off in a room or area of its own, but not to the extent of complete isolation or exclusiveness.

Office furniture

Having settled on location and general lay-out, the next major considerations are the furnishings to accommodate the system and the overall workplace design. Appendix 1 gives some help on sources of information which will help identify appropriate suppliers. This is the area where poor planning can be the cause of much of the operator discomfort, fatigue, annoyance and eventual lowering of morale mentioned at the beginning of the chapter. Postural fatigue results from pro-longed use of a VDU without the scope for adjustment. Common symptoms range from aching head, neck, lower back and shoulders to pain in the lower joints and knees, as well as loss of sensation from various parts of the body (due to impaired blood flow). Specific

causes include: inadequate knee clearance; wrong working level (defined as the distance between the underside of the thighs and the palms of the hands); unfavourable angle for forearms and wrists; stress on the back and leg muscles; unfavourable inclination or twisting of the head; sideways body move-ment; and unfavourable viewing distances for the screen and source documents.

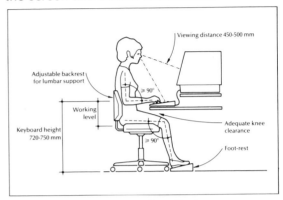

Recommended posture and positioning

Workstation Table

A workstation needs something to sit on and any old table will not do! Just the screen and keyboard may need to be accommodated, but sometimes also the disc drives and processor are designed to sit alongside these. The table should be able to accommodate operators' working papers on either side of the keyboard. Where the keyboard is separate from the screen, attached to it via a short cable, full advantage should be taken of the scope for moving the screen back to suit operator preferences for viewing distance. It should also be possible to move the keyboard to one side so that source documents can be placed on a stand (document holder) directly behind the keyboard when a document is first being typed. The operator needs only an occasional glance at the screen during this activity. Such an arrangement avoids un-favourable twisting of the head otherwise caused by looking sideways at the document. Depending on the positioning of equipment, it may be desirable for the table to have a modesty panel to provide privacy for the operator.

Suppliers can provide purpose-built desks and tables but some designs do not take into account the factors just discussed. Tables are available that allow separate adjustment of the keyboard or screen height, the former being more important for achieving the correct working level. Also available now are portable turntables for angling and rotating VDU's. You should consult independent furniture suppliers to see what they have to offer. Your word processing supplier will have a limited range, and almost certainly it will have been bought-in from another company. You may decide that it is worth additional investment in something from one of the specialist firms who now market individually tailored workplaces. (Such firms often refer to these as workstations rather than our use of the word which refers to the equipment). Whatever is chosen, remember the point made earlier about matt surfaces to reduce glare and reflection.

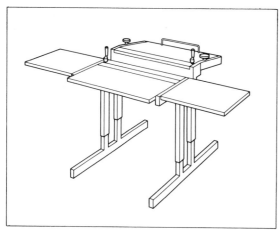

Specimen workstation table

Some VDU tables have a recess in which the VDU sits at a slightly lower level than the rest of the work surface. If the engineers need to get to the back of the VDU but cannot easily do so because of the general lay-out of the system, then they will have to swivel it round. Even with a pivoting screen this may be awkward if a table with a recess is used. Recessed tables may also limit the scope for suitable positioning of the keyboard. Whatever table is chosen it needs to be solid enough to take the weight of the VDU, keyboard, and possibly disc drives and processor, although equipment is now significantly lighter than the early models. Appropriate information about dimensions and weight ought to be included in the specification made available to you, to help in deciding on furniture.

Seating

Chair design is of critical importance in avoiding postural fatigue. The chair height must be easily adjustable.

The backrest should be easily adjustable in angle as well as in height. There should be good support for the lower back and thighs with surfaces of the backrest curving smoothly outwards to avoid cutting into the body. But there is no point in having such flexibility if operators are not also instructed in how to adjust their position, and made aware of the benefits of adopting good posture at the workstation.

Chairs should be on castors so that operators can readily move in and out from the VDU. The material should be rough textured and flexible rather than shiny and hard to help stabilise the sitting position and avoid pressure spots. There are many designs of chair now on the market that take into account these points, some being considerably more expensive than others. Remember to have adequate seating for those visiting the installation or consulting with operators.

Printer Table

We mentioned earlier that it is preferable to have the printer on a table of its own. If continuous or carrier stationery is to be used, it is sensible to use a table designed for the purpose, with a cage at the back to catch the output and possibly a tray or support for the pile of stationery being fed in.

Floppy Disc Drives

The disc drives may be integrated with the VDU housing, may come as a stand-alone desk-top unit, may require to be housed in a free-standing floor unit, or in one that is integral with a purpose-built desk. Some furniture suppliers now offer optional housing units that can be fitted to their tables or desks as required. If these are chosen, ensure the ventilation grill is in an appropriate position. Any free-standing unit should be situated in such a way that the drive doors are readily accessible and within arm's reach of the operator. Wherever the disc drive unit is placed it should not be prone to accidental knocking by the operator or passers-by.

If considering placing the printer on a free-standing floor unit that houses the drives (not directly on top of them), check with your supplier that the vibrations from the printer will be adequately absorbed not to affect drive operation.

Additional Storage Facilities

Maintaining a general air of tidiness around the system by the provision of suitable storage units helps efficiency, protects consumable items, and maximises work space for operators. Some suggestions are given. Bear in mind also that bulk ordering of consumables may require storage space in addition to that mentioned.

Print Elements. It is likely that a site with a daisywheel or Spinwriter printer will invest in a variety of typestyles. Print elements need to be accessible and stored in a unit to keep them tidy. Special storage boxes can be purchased but it may be possible to improvise with other boxes. (Wheels and thimbles are supplied in individual protective cases which should be retained if not investing in a special storage unit).

Ribbons. If the site varies the type of ribbon used, a stock of these needs to be readily accessible and again stored in a box or tray for protection as well as ready access. If refillable cartridges are used, a container for spent cartridges needs to be kept close-at-hand. Provided it does not get in the way of leg movement, a storage pedestal underneath or fitted to the operator's desk can be used for immediate supplies of ribbons, print elements and even to accommodate a small floppy disc library. But it is preferable to have these stored at a more suitable level in relation to the printer and disc drives to save frequent bending down.

Stationery. Because of the paper consumption of the system, (due to ease of redrafting and generally greater output), it is advisable to have a local stationery cupboard to house adequate stocks of paper supply.

Floppy Disc Library Cupboard. Readers are referred to Chapter 8 for discussion of storage facilities for floppy disc libraries, but it may be necessary for security reasons to lock the floppy disc library in a cupboard each night, if a lockable storage unit is not regarded as adequate.

Sundry Items

Just as typists are provided with stationery tidys and work-trays to help organise their workload, such items should not be forgotten when planning the installation of a word processor. There are other items that need to be considered. Some of these should be available at the time of installation, others can be acquired as the organisation around the system takes shape.

Work-trays. In addition to "In" and "Out" trays, trays may be needed to file work completed but still to be printed, and for work scheduled to be done at times when the operator is unlikely to be interrupted or has to use different software such as utilities. If a number of operators frequently use the system, each one may want their own set of trays so that they do not have to take their work away with them.

Document Holders. To avoid unfavourable inclination of the head and uncomfortable

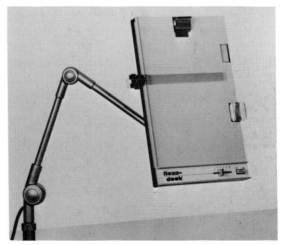

Document holder (courtesy of Perforag)

body rotation when referring from document to the screen, document or copy holders can be beneficial. A variety of designs are available to suit individual preferences, nature of the source documents and the work. Documents may generally be neat or they may be messy with lots of insertions and notes, involve odd paper sizes, or require the operator to add notes and make marks on them. Certain designs of holder will be more suitable than others to each of these. It is preferable to be able to adjust the inclination and possibly height of the holder. The more expensive have foot controls for moving a magnifying ruler line down the page. Some provide slots for holding pages dealt with. Whatever the level of investment decided upon, the final choice should rest with those using them.

Ready Paper Supply. Particularly for manual single-feed stationery operation, the operator needs ready access to a supply of stationery. One possibility, if the printer is next to a wall, is to mount a rack on the wall just above the printer. There needs to be a generous **waste-paper-basket** to hand – there will inevitably be discards from the printer to get rid of.

Reference Works. All reference or procedures manuals relating to the system should be readily accessible and may require a local shelf-unit.

Foot-rests. Particularly for short operators, a foot-rest designed for office use may be advisable as a further aid to comfort. These also have the advantage that they can prevent floor scuffing and localised carpet wear. To allow adjustment of the angle of tilt to suit individual requirements, it is better to get one with an adjustable rake between 10° and 15°. Height should also be adjustable between 0 mm and 50 mm.

Notice-board. It is convenient to display frequently used telephone numbers of support staff, maintenance engineers and consumable suppliers, as well as other reminders on a notice-board near to the system. Operators may design their own wall charts to list routines for switching equipment on and off and using utilities, and they may wish to display charts of print element designs.

Checklist 9

The Location and its Environment:

☐ lighting – positioning of the screen is critical, consider general illumination, task lighting, glare and reflection;

☐ heat and humidity – word processing systems generate heat, keep humidity to 40%– 60%R.H.;

☐ noise is generated by the printer, cooling fans, keyboard click and system bleeps, think about others in the vicinity as well as the operators;

☐ space requirements – allow room for operators to access equipment, move around during rest pauses, and for visitors;

☐ electrical requirements – ensure there are plenty of sockets, and check mains supply, requirements for a shared or distributed logic system will be a major planning exercise involving the supplier and building staff;

☐ static electricity – ensure equipment is properly earthed, if static is a problem preventative measures may be required.

Lay-out:

1. Operators need frequent access to the printer.

2. There should be safe access to all sockets.

3. A telephone should be within arms' reach.

4. There will be restrictions on equipment cable length.

5. Engineers may need to get to the back of equipment.

6. There should be adequate clearance behind the printer.

7. The printer vibrates and is better on a separate table.

8. Provide additional work surfaces.

9. Reference or training installations should be given a degree of privacy.

Office Furniture:

☐ workstation table – purpose built tables and VDU turntables are available;

☐ chair design is of critical importance;

☐ purpose-built tables are available for printers using continuous stationery;

☐ housing units may need to be purchased for disc drives;

☐ additional storage facilities are recommended for consumables, stationery and may be required for locking away the disc library;

☐ a number of sundry items may be required – work-trays, document holders, ready paper supply, additional waste-paper baskets, a local shelf-unit for reference works, foot-rests, a notice-board.

Whatever the investment in workplace design, rest pauses should be encouraged.

Responsibilities and System Operation

Responsibilities

The supervisor
Operators
Originators

Organisation of the disc library

Work scheduling and system use

Work transfer
Day-to-day scheduling
"Cafeteria" or bureau service
Emergency arrangements
Logging throughput

Security aspects

Security of disc and document access
Security of system access
Flood and fire precautions
Security against corruption or loss of data

Maintenance

Hardware and consumables
Software

Establishing procedures

Checklist

The first part of this chapter discusses the responsibilities required of those operating and supervising the equipment. It then goes on to look at the organisation and procedures associated with running a system. Much of this will be carried out by the person in charge of the day-to-day running of the word processing equipment. But in successfully appointing someone to this position, you need to be aware of what is involved in the job. Under some headings, therefore, a brief summary is given, with detailed considerations of interest to that individual provided in Appendix 2.

Responsibilities

When talking about centralisation versus decentralisation of word processing facilities within an organisation, we intimated that the initial tendency was for job specialisation in the operation of equipment. But now the use of word processing systems is becoming an additional skill to support existing job functions and not just of secretaries but administrators, authors, and engineers. This is a trend that will continue as office automation develops, the overall objective being increased efficiency and effectiveness from the office as one integrated human and technological system.

The future role of typists and secretaries is a key factor and must be given serious consideration in this first step in office automation. There will still be a need for specialists in word processing operation who are well versed in the capabilities of particular systems, but there are many installations where word processors are successfully shared by secretaries who still fulfill many other duties. And indeed, word processing should allow secretaries to carry out their typing tasks more efficiently, so freeing them to take on additional responsibilities.

However, no matter what equipment is used, someone needs to have overall responsibility for running it, whether as part of a large integrated network of word processors or an isolated, dedicated stand-alone system. It may be just one of many responsibilities held. If such responsibility is not assigned, the outcome is likely to be inefficient and less than maximum use of the system. For our purposes we shall refer to such an individual as the supervisor. With a large network of systems there is more likely to be a word processing manager appointed with perhaps a number of supervisors reporting to him or her. In a small business the person may be the only one who uses the system.

The Supervisor

The role of the supervisor is especially important in the early days of installation, for such an individual can provide the driving force behind a system's acceptance. If also acting in a training capacity, the individual will have an impact on the ease and speed with which others begin to use the equipment, thus the organisation as a whole begins to derive significant benefits. This section of Chapter 10 concentrates on the responsibilities to be assumed by such a person – or they may be shared, with one person having ultimate responsibility. In the case of a small shared logic system the post may even be a full-time job and ideally should be filled by someone with previous technical experience, so that they understand the more complicated aspects of such equipment.

System Expertise. Anyone adopting a supervisory role needs to quickly become thoroughly conversant in the operation of the system. They need to try out enhancements and ensure that other users are aware of, and learn how to use these. In discussion with operators, originators and managers, they should be able to recommend application areas for new features introduced by the supplier as well as assess the implications on any current modes of working.

System Responsibilities. Some of the areas listed have been mentioned in a different context elsewhere in the book, others new to the reader are covered in more detail later in this chapter. This section serves to point out that someone needs to assume responsibility for them.

1. Organisation of the disc library.

2. Ordering consumable items (print elements, ribbons, floppy discs and stationery), and advising on the use of these. Awareness of new products and competitive prices, and looking at the possibilities for bulk purchasing.

3. Advising on and organising the purchase of sundry items such as document holders, and ancillary equipment such as acoustic hood, tractor-feed, and single-sheet feeder, if the purchase of these has been postponed until after the installation.

4. Maintenance, security and fault practices, as well as ensuring that building services staff (a) know what to do in the event of a workstation unintentionally being left on overnight, and (b) are aware of the need to alert the installation before power supplies are switched off (to mend fuses), so that the system can first be closed down to avoid disc corruption.

5. Advise on enhancements to the environment while ensuring that current standards are maintained.

6. Establishing, teaching and documenting any required guidelines, procedures or practices concerning use of the equipment.

7. Establishing and maintaining a rapport with the sales, support and engineering staff of the system supplier.

8. Monitoring use of the system.

Work Organisation. The supervisor should be responsible for work scheduling and possibly shared use of the system, with appropriate procedures for logging work in and out if necessary, and will need to arbitrate in times of conflict in work scheduling.

Personnel Responsibilities. The supervisor needs to assume responsibility for the day-to-day supervision of operating staff. Responsibilities may include training new users and assisting in a familiarisation programme for managers and originators.

Word Processing Expertise. The supervisor should maintain an awareness of developments in word processing, reading relevant periodicals and texts and should represent the organisation on any User Groups (i.e. Customer Associations) for the system.

Operators

Some operators will become far more experienced than others and the speed of learning will vary tremendously. Managers and other staff may also learn to use the system. In general experienced operators should have the following responsibilities.

1. Understand the basic concepts of how the system operates – this is necessary to ensure they realise the importance of following procedures.

2. Interpret information about the state of the system, which is readily displayed to them on the screen as messages or prompts.

3. Know and apply all the features of the system so that maximum benefit can be derived from it in the "processing of words".

4. Remain calm, clear-thinking and coherent in error and problem situations and as far as possible be able to take corrective action.

Originators

Originators will need to get to know and adhere to certain procedures or practices that will help operators and smooth the running of the system. This is covered in Chapter 11 on "Training and Staff Selection".

Organisation of the disc library

A "system" will be required for the organisation of the disc library and for ensuring that originators as well as operators maintain records of what documents are called and where they are held in the library, i.e. on which floppy disc or in which section of a hard disc(s). The library system needs to include any archived media. Just as inadequate paper filing systems waste people's time and hamper productivity and effectiveness, so does failure to devise and maintain an adequate system for word processing files. Because the information is invisible to the human eye the situation is exacerbated and can lead to chaos.

Any system devised should be clearly documented and made known to all users. It needs to cover disc and document naming, disc filing, maintenance of disc indexes, and document records. These aspects are covered in more detail in Appendix 2.

Work scheduling and system use

Work Transfer

Having organised the siting of the system, its fixtures and fittings, and the acquisition of ancillary equipment, the conversion of the workload needs to be planned. It is good sense to apply the more straightforward documents first to allow staff to become familiar with the equipment. More involved work can then be contemplated, using some of the more sophisticated and demanding facilities. Operators and originators should be encouraged to experiment with documents. Some lay-outs that initially appear difficult might turn out to be quite straightforward to accommodate, others may require a re-think of the originator's approach. Such experiments need to be accommodated in planning work transfer.

The person in charge of the system should also be aware of what enhancements to the software are in the pipeline from a supplier. It may be that some documents will be better dealt with by a forthcoming release of software that has additional facilities particularly suited to the task. In this case their conversion to the system could be better left till that time. A supervisor should not hesitate to contact the supplier for help – the supplier may know of ways round what seems to be a limitation in use of the software. It might also spark-off food for thought in terms of enhancements not yet planned by the supplier.

There may be jobs that are just as, or even more efficiently done on a typewriter and do not need to be transferred to a word processor in the foreseeable future. It may be necessary to state policy with regard to such documents, if the equipment is likely to be used to capacity fairly quickly.

Day-to-day Scheduling

It is likely that much of the work for which the system will be used will be of a recurring nature – for example the updating of regular reports. Operators should be able to organise their work to take account of these regular updating sessions. Originators can be encouraged to submit copy well in advance of publication deadlines where work is put together piece-meal.

There are times when a number of similar

tasks are better done together or at appropriate times in the day. This may relate to printing activities, confidentiality of the work, the floppy discs being used, the use of separate software, or to activities that are best left to non-interruptive periods. These activities include tidying discs (getting rid of documents no longer needed), copying documents between discs, copying complete discs, or formatting discs ready to be used as work discs.

We introduced above the concept of scheduling printing activities. The sequence in which jobs are printed in an installation with a heavy output of printed pages can require a great deal of attention. It may be preferable to schedule all jobs using the same stationery together (whether using a tractor-feed or single-sheet feeder). Some jobs may tie-up the printer for a long time, others may require a change of typestyle, some may prove noisier than others and are better left to a more tolerable period in the day. (If there is much dense text, many rulings, or excessive bold printing, the noise generated by the printer increases noticeably).

If the system is shared with others, or used on a "hired-time" basis (discussed next), operators will probably want to work on it for a significant time-slot. Inevitably, at the end of the period they will want to use the printer. If the printer is shared between workstations it is advisable not to have matching time-slots.

All such aspects need to be taken into consideration in organising work on ,the system. Where a number of staff are involved, each installation is advised to establish its own pattern and if necessary to document some basic guidelines for work scheduling. Scheduling may also involve controlling managers and originators who find it convenient to do some of their own input and editing. It may be necessary to watch that they are using their time efficiently and not using the machine solely because they have become "hooked" on the system (just as some may have initially feared the consequences of operators becoming preoccupied with the system).

"Cafeteria" or Bureau Service
Although this section is more relevant to a large organisation, small businesses may also find it of interest if there is spare capacity on their system and they are prepared to contemplate making it available to people outside the company. As we indicated above it may be that equipment is shared by a number of departments or different sections within a department. This is sometimes referred to as a "cafeteria" operation. A booking system will have to be introduced to ensure fairness and efficient use. This is something that can be organised by the supervisor, although it is likely to call for considerable diplomacy in some situations involving managers and other originators as well as operators. With a shared system, it is advisable to start straight away with a formal booking scheme or to at least give plenty of warning that one is to be introduced.

It may be that an internal charging system is introduced for use of the equipment. One department may have paid for the system on the understanding that other users are prepared to pay on an ad hoc use basis. The supervisor may be required to look after charging arrangements and perhaps set pricing policy with management. It may also be that any spare operator capacity from within the department can be offered as part of the service. Whether the system is charged for or not in a "cafeteria" or shared situation, the cost of consumables needs to be taken into account. Will users be expected to bring their own or will the department responsible for the system provide them? If so, and a charging system operates, how will these be charged for? Will everything be itemised or only where use of ribbons and paper is excessive? How often will charges for the use of the system be levied? Would it be better to make an annual charge related to a department's overall use of the word processor? Where charging is introduced, it is important to keep records to ensure that charges are accurate and queries from customers can be satisfied. One further issue to be decided is whether users must first be vetted for ability to use the system unsupervised.

Emergency Arrangements
There will inevitably be occasions when the system will be down (inoperable) for an impractical period. Alternative arrangements will have to be made for completing outstanding work. This may involve use of some other

department's system or a bureau, some of the work may have to be rescheduled, or some carried out on a typewriter, or a combination of these. Such eventualities need to be planned for. Establishing a rapport with other local sites (internal or external to the company) and coming to some informal agreement for providing back-up facilities for each other may prove a wise move. Even if such arrangements only cover use of the printer, they can be well worth developing, as you may find the printer gives more trouble than the rest of the equipment. If it is just the printer that has gone wrong, other work can still be done on your system, using another site's equipment to print out material. This need not interfere too much with their operation provided their configuration has enough floppy disc drives.

Specific contingency plans ought to be made for regularly published documents likely to be affected. It may be that a typewriter could be used to update a hard-copy version of the previous issue of a document that alters only slightly each time. But if so, it is as well to see that the typeface normally used matches that of the stand-by typewriter.

Logging Throughput

In the early days of an installation it is worth recording the number of hours being spent on the system and by whom. Try and devise some painless method of also recording document throughput (a paper count keeping track of clean paper used, waste, and discarded drafts gives a rough order of magnitude of total pages printed as well as final copy). More stringent methods may be required where an organisation-and-methods department is involved. Even for the office that has independently acquired its word processor, some measure of use of the system is prudent. This anticipates questions from visitors or other departments, from managers at budget time if the system has to be continually justified, and helps in budgeting the operation, or planning for another system.

Care is needed in the method chosen otherwise operators may feel the subject of a time-and-motion study. Generally staff do not mind logging time for specific pieces of work, if it provides a means of letting an originator know how long a poorly scripted document

or extensive editing has taken! Where operator time is charged for as part of a bureau service, logging time will be mandatory.

Security aspects

Security of Disc and Document Access

On some systems documents can be held securely through the use of passwords. An alternative is to lock away the disc library or appropriate parts of it each night. Some of the work carried out on a system may be secure in terms of confidentiality. The work may have to be scheduled accordingly (with no others around or only those appropriately vetted). Alternatively, if visitors or other staff are likely to be in view of the system, special furniture screens may have to be erected around the operators for privacy at these times. Turning down the brightness of the VDU to almost unreadable levels is one way of coping with casual glances from those around the system at the original keying in stage, since the typist hardly needs to refer to the screen.

Security of System Access

It may be that the system is not to be used without supervisory staff present, in which case the room in which it is housed could be locked or, if in an open-plan situation, it may be necessary to find some other means of "locking" it. One way is to use a password to the system disc if the software offers this facility. But system disc passwords in a multi-installation environment do not cover for others coming along with their own system disc and using the equipment. Another alternative is the availability of a key or similar device required to switch on the equipment. In general, however, we hope such needs are rare as they limit the scope for encouraging the wide use of word processing facilities within an organisation, and for promoting the concept of word processing as an additional tool to be exploited by all.

Flood and Fire Precautions

If security precautions are taken for normal office files against hazards such as fire or water damage (e.g. the use of special filing cabinets), similar precautions may have to be employed for data held on floppies.

Security Against Corruption or Loss of Data

Corruption and/or loss of data on floppies can

arise either at the document or disc level, and may be due to direct operator error or some external accident. Those in charge of a system need to consider with originators the various types of corruption and data loss that could occur, to assess the likelihood of occurrence and the impact on the workload. These then need to be weighed against the effort involved in taking the necessary precautions. On the basis of that assessment the extent to which special security measures have to be taken should be decided and guidelines documented.

Disc corruption can be handled by a supplier's software support organisation, although they may not be able to retrieve all the data. Before sending the disc for recovery work, it may be possible to take a copy of the material not affected by the corruption. Note that such a service may not be available if you have opted for a word processing package to run on a microcomputer, or if so, only at considerable cost.

The standard method for coping with these eventualities, in particular disc corruption, is to take a *security copy* on another disc especially when documents have involved much preparation or cannot readily be regenerated. Or a regularly updated document not necessarily long or complicated, may have a sufficiently vital publication deadline that sending a corrupted disc off to your support people for a few days could not be tolerated. Individual documents may be copied or the complete disc.

Another form of security usually applicable to system discs on which the supplier allows you to store or write documents is the use of read/write stickers. (Other suppliers completely protect their system discs before releasing them.) This facility is also typical of discs for microcomputer systems. The stickers are placed over a purpose-designed notch in the protective jacket of the floppy. For 5¼ inch discs, when the sticker is present the disc cannot be written on, when peeled off it can. For 8 inch discs the converse is true i.e. the sticker must be present before the disc can be written on.

Possible *causes of data loss* that need to be considered are:

□ an operator amends the wrong (but similar) document;

□ an operator mistakenly alters or erases all or part of a document;

□ an operator formats or disc copies onto the wrong disc;

□ corruption by a system "crash", power failure, or switching equipment off or on with discs in position;

□ corruption by physical mishandling (the disc gets scratched, buckled, or contaminated by dust, coffee, ash);

□ a disc corruption caused during manufacture that does not show up until the system tries to write on the corrupted track;

□ loss or theft.

As already suggested security measures involve additional disciplines, time and costs whether it be keeping discs under lock and key, use of passwords or taking secure copies (at disc or document level). Other points on security are care in the naming of discs and documents, so that data is not mistakenly accessed and altered; also, copying of documents before updating them (unless the system automatically does this for you), and only when satisfied with the edited document, is the previous version deleted.

When security copies (of documents or complete discs) are being kept, they should be taken after every major update and ideally should not be copied to overwrite the previous security copy, in case something drastic happens during the operation. For example the operator may wrongly write the old security copy of a disc over the current version instead of vice versa. Similarly, if only the document is being copied to another disc, then every time such a copy is taken for security reasons, it should be as a new document on the second disc before deleting the previous security copy.

Maintenance

A word processing system is a costly item that deserves care and attention given the extensive use that will be made of it. Formal maintenance contract matters were covered in Chapter 7, but there are a number of practices and procedures that should be followed by those using the system, to maintain everything in good condition, minimise problems and maximise use. Remember, when the system goes down it can impact a significant number of people within the organisation, or if a floppy disc gets contaminated a number of hours work may have been totally wasted.

Hardware and Consumables
There are a variety of practices that should be adopted in looking after the hardware and consumables. These are covered in Appendix 2. In addition the supervisor should be responsible for maintaining consumable supplies and therefore form an awareness of patterns of usage and likely changes in future needs.

Software
Any major faults will require assistance from the supplier or support organisation. However, there may also be times when situations arise that cannot readily be explained by staff. These should similarly be reported in case they are the outcome of a fault (bug) in the software. It is important in any fault or potential fault situation to ascertain and note exactly the events that led up to it to assist interpretation of the problem.

It is not necessary to immediately report relatively trivial faults but operators may be encouraged to register details if a tray, book or similar provision is available. This can also be used to note possible enhancements to the system or handy tips that often come to mind or are tried out when the operator is in the middle of a job. The easier it is for staff to make a quick note of these and dispose of it, the more likely they are to oblige. Whatever means is provided, if more than one person uses the system, someone has to have the responsibility for checking the comments tray or book on a regular basis and taking appropriate action (faults and possible enhancements notified and tips recorded in the user guide for the system as well as generally made aware to all users).

Establishing procedures
Part of the effort to ensure successful running of the system and to assist operators and other users involves establishing procedures, standards, rules of operation, and courses of action in certain eventualities, and to formally document these. In an office environment where activities and methods have tended to be of an ad hoc nature this exercise will be far from trivial, but it is vital if maximum benefit is to be derived from the investment. It will provide a sound basis for further developments in office automation. This is not to suggest that the office becomes regimented, just as important is the way procedures are introduced and staff made to appreciate the benefits of following them.

A list of items that should be considered for incorporation in guidance notes or clearly defined procedures is given in Appendix 2.

Checklist 10

Responsibilities:

- [ ] the supervisor needs to be thoroughly conversant with the system as well as hold specific responsibilities concerning the organisation of the system, work organisation, personnel, and word processing expertise;

- [ ] operators should understand how the system operates, interpret messages and prompts, be skilled in using the system's features and facilities, and be able to take corrective action in error and problem situations.

Organisation of the Disc Library: a system needs to be devised and documented.

Work Scheduling and System Use:

- [ ] work transfer needs to be planned;

- [ ] day-to-day scheduling involves planning for regular document update sessions, grouping similar tasks, demands on the printer, and possibly sharing use of the system;

- [ ] spare capacity may be hired out on a "cafeteria" or bureau basis requiring additional system organisation and management;

- [ ] alternative arrangements should be made for coping with system unavailability in emergencies;

- [ ] a method should be devised for logging throughput of the system.

Security Aspects: consider the types of corruption and data loss that could occur and weigh these against the effort involved in taking the necessary precautions. In particular, consider:

- [ ] security of disc and document access;

- [ ] security of system access;

- [ ] flood and fire precautions;

- [ ] security against corruption or loss of data.

Maintenance: A number of practices and procedures should be followed with respect to:

- [ ] hardware and consumables;

- [ ] software.

Establishing Procedures: procedures, standards, rules of operation, and set courses of action should be established and documented.

Training and Staff Selection

Familiarisation

We have deliberately left this topic until this stage so that you come to it appreciating the extent to which new knowledge, understanding and skills have to be acquired by staff. We hope also by now it is apparent to readers that much of the key to success lies in the preparation and training of all those likely to become involved in using the equipment or affected by its use. In Chapter 7 we talked about the provision of formal training courses by suppliers. We suggested that the common approach adopted by first-time users is to send one or two staff on such a course, then to rely on these people to train others within the organisation. But long before this stage, staff need to be briefed about what word processing is, what is being contemplated, what the objectives are, the effect it is likely to have on their work, and their comments invited.

Many potential operators are nervous and apprehensive at the idea of word processing. It is vital at this early stage to *dispel the common fears* of:

- [ ] potential redundancy;
- [ ] loss of skills;
- [ ] concern at being able to cope and to learn how to use the equipment; and
- [ ] potential lowering in the standard of work submitted, with increased number of revisions required.

Where a centralised pool is being proposed or jobs are being specialised, further reservations may be observed:

- [ ] loss of status because staff are no longer considered as personal secretaries;
- [ ] the possibility of being stuck at the keyboard all day;
- [ ] lack of continuity in seeing a job through from start to finish, loss of contact between originators and typists; and
- [ ] fear of general isolation.

In most cases operators, once trained and totally familiar with equipment, look back and laugh at their original doubts and fears about their ability to cope with the situation. But the fact that these and the other concerns mentioned do exist, affects their initial attitude and reaction, and must be attended to from the outset.

Just as important is the ***orientation of originators and senior management***. The latter may not be directly affected from a work point-of-view, but their backing and support for the operation are fundamental to its success. Managers and other originators can experience misapprehension and fears at the prospect of word processing just like operators can:

☐ managers envisage their secretary will not always be as close to hand if the system is sited in another office;

☐ worry about security of information (loss and confidentiality);

☐ concern at operators becoming preoccupied with the system and not devoting enough attention to other responsibilities;

☐ anticipation of demands for more remuneration by operators in return for additional skills and particularly in a large organisation, associated industrial relations problems.

If adequate familiarisation is not carried out then many problems can stem from originators once the system has been installed. These relate to abuse of the word processor. Originators may expect faster turnround than is realistic. They may make excessive demands concerning alterations and the number of redrafts. System organisation needs to be discussed in the early days of familiarisation, to ensure that managers and staff are fully aware of all the implications, and can contribute to the planning activities associated with the installation and re-organisation of office duties. Staff orientation should help to identify the enthusiastic and progressive members of staff who can play a more active role and be relied upon to encourage the more doubtful.

What steps can be taken to successfully familiarise staff in the manner we have been discussing? There are three sets of activities which we suggest you consider, based on past success in a number of organisations: seminars, visits, and involvement in the equipment selection process. Even where the office is small and close-knit so that all staff tend to be aware of most of what is going on, it is advisable to take positive steps to show that the entire issue is being approached with all seriousness and attention to the "people" aspects. It is suggested, therefore, that where only a handful of staff are involved, the following recommendations are paid heed to but tailored accordingly.

Seminars. All staff affected whether managers, executives, technicians, professionals, secretaries, typists, clerks, or administrators can be called together in small group(s) for a few hours, perhaps even a day, in the form of a seminar. Presentations can cover the following areas.

1. Introduction by management to outline activities to date.

2. The fundamentals of word processing:
   ☐ what it is
   ☐ terminology
   ☐ equipment
   ☐ what it can do
   ☐ applications.

3. Demonstration of equipment and hands-on experience.

4. The impact on originators and the organisation of the office. Perhaps this session can be supplemented by an established user's experience.

5. Management's objectives and future plans.

6. Discussion session to answer queries, overcome misapprehensions and identify the organisational implications.

Arranging speakers and a demonstration will be much easier if you have already decided on a supplier, but if your potential investment is significant enough you may be able to enlist the help of a supplier who has not yet won the business. It may not be possible to arrange for a demonstration if a seminar is carried out on your own premises, in which case a selection of staff should be allowed to attend one later at a supplier's premises.

Visits. To further overcome secretarial and

typists' concerns arrange for staff to visit other word processing sites to talk with experienced operators and have the opportunity to sit down and try out a system.

Involvement in Equipment Selection. Involving potential operators in equipment selection as well as representatives of those whose work will be carried out on the system, has the following advantages:

1. It helps familiarisation with word processing.

2. Their experience and knowledge of the workload will be valuable in specifying requirements and assessing equipment.

3. Involvement improves morale.

4. An active rather than a passive role helps dispel fears and reservations at the thought of change.

5. It can help typists and originators better understand each other's position, and lead to a healthy rapport once equipment is installed.

Operator and supervisor training

If purchasing a ***dedicated word processor*** it is likely that you will opt for what is offered by the supplier in the way of training, whether a formal course, self-teach or audio package. In some cases further courses specifically geared towards advanced facilities and/or supervisors will also be available. If not, then training someone to supervisor level to assume the responsibilities we have already outlined may involve management time (with the aid of this text and additional background reading of appropriate word processing journals – some guidance is given in Appendix 1). As mentioned in Chapter 7 some of the polytechnics and colleges are now offering courses many of which cover the general principles of word processing. Some word processing bureaux also run courses on a number of dedicated word processors.

One oft quoted criticism of suppliers' courses is the lack of orientation towards applications relevant to attendees' workload. If there are enough operators to be given formal training in this way, then it may be worth the additional investment of getting the supplier to customise a course for your organisation.

If you opt for a ***word processing package on a micro*** then the scope for formal training is considerably limited. Once again some polytechnics, word processing bureaux, as well as consultancies and other independent training organisations offer training in these, or your supplier may offer some courses. Otherwise it is very much a case of sitting down with a training manual and teaching yourself. What is available in the way of formal training, therefore, may figure strongly in your selection criteria for a package.

Independent training establishments can provide courses over an extended period of time rather than on an intensive basis, the problem with the latter being that staff tend to feel "thrown in at the deep end" and try to remember too much. The result is exhaustion and confusion. Nonetheless once staff return to the office and begin to work with the system, the initial training course begins to seem less of a nightmare, with useful information having registered and beginning to mean something.

How quickly staff become proficient once doing live work depends on the individual, the extent to which they are given time to experiment and consult the manual, the availability of an experienced operator to provide assistance, and the quality of reference documentation provided on how to use the system. All too often originators expect staff to return from courses and be totally conversant with the system and to catch up on the backlog of work while trying out all manner of applications. It will pay in the end to see that ***trainees have ample time*** to try out and register what they have learned and to experiment with documents. This could involve taking on temporary staff to cover for them in the meantime.

Once one or two staff become competent operators, provided they are reasonably adept at explaining and enjoy teaching others, then ***in-house training*** is a viable approach. The advantage is that staff can be paced according to individual requirements and tuition can be on a one-to-one basis. There is no reason why those first trained should be restricted to typists. There may be some advantage in having an office manager or similar senior member of a department assume this role, particularly if he or she has been leading the preparation and equipment selection project. Some guidelines for anyone assuming the role of in-house trainer and not formally trained to teach are given later in this chapter.

Scheduling formal training is critical. There is no point in having staff attend a course weeks in advance of the installation of equipment, for they will have forgotten most of what they learned. Worries and concerns may also return in the intervening period. Some buyers try and arrange courses to coincide with the installation, but a gap of just a few days in advance can be an advantage if trainees are provided with manuals to consult in the meantime. Once live use of the system begins it is better to start with fairly simple tasks, and to attempt more complicated operations as confidence in the system and people's abilities build up.

Establishing a rapport with other user sites whether within the same or different organisations can be a tremendous help in attempting to use new features or clarify points of confusion. User Groups (i.e. Customer Associations) can be helpful in identifying other sites and may publish a regular bulletin with useful tips and advice. Ideally, suppliers should be able to provide such assistance but this type of post-implementation support is not always readily available.

On-going training needs to be planned. In a larger organisation, once immediate users of the system have been trained, provision could be made for training other interested secretarial and typing staff. These staff may see scope for one or two applications in their area not before considered. Or it may anticipate future needs for another system to be installed elsewhere within the organisation. Or the staff may prove a useful source of back-up operators.

Training for new staff joining the department will also need to be planned for. As further releases of software are made or additional applications software becomes available, staff will need to try these out and learn how to use any new features.

Originator training

Those submitting the work also need orientation if not formal training when equipment is introduced, to help get the most out of what the system has to offer and to assist those operating it. They will need to understand and learn to **adapt to new procedures and practices** and to change previous habits. For example in marking-up what used to be a final typed document with small corrections, originators would normally use pencil and write lightly to avoid a retype. With word processing all corrections should be clearly marked in a different colour to help the operator quickly locate them, since the entire page can readily be printed again once the corrections are done. Another example is to strictly avoid cutting-and-pasting edited material, since this makes it difficult for the operator to relate what is already held on disc to the edited draft.

Some originators seem to think that because a document has been word processed this allows them to virtually re-write it. In such instances it is just as efficient to rekey the new version from scratch! Originators need to realise that word processing does not mean that they can become sloppy in their document preparation in this way. However, they may find that they can provide a rougher copy to a typist than before, because the typist now knows that extensive editing (within reason) will still allow them to produce a well-presented document without the need for a complete retype. Originators may notice significant benefits in this respect with regard to efficient use of their time, but such demands on the operator call for a very healthy rapport between the two. In particular, the operator needs to appreciate the overall increased efficiency and effectiveness to the organisation that results from such teamwork, and the originator needs to show adequate appreciation of the operator's efforts.

Originators will need to learn to make use of the facility for submitting work before it is completed, where this involves inserted rather than heavily amended text. In this way peaks in the workload may be smoothed and pressure to meet last minute deadlines avoided. While word processing means that originators should no longer be hesitant about asking for another draft, they may have to be discouraged from making trivial changes where no significant benefits will be achieved in terms of the written communication.

Much of the above is learned as the

organisation around a system develops and can be highly dependent on the supervisor establishing the right sort of relationship with those involved. But some indications of what is required of originators should have been given in earlier familiarisation exercises. Once the system is installed, if originators have the opportunity to learn at least the basics of how to operate the system, they are more likely to develop a productive rapport with staff doing their work. This can be just as important a part of any in-house training programme as training secretaries and typists. The work of some organisations may be such that there are positive advantages to be gained from executives and other staff doing some of their own editing or even first input on the system. But care is needed that they do not let fascination for operating it impede efficiency and effectiveness.

It is important too that management play their part by being seen to make use of the system and adhere to any new procedures or practices established.

Guidelines for in-house trainers

The decision to assign the role of trainer to someone who has not been trained to teach *should not be taken lightly*. Just because someone knows how to operate the equipment does not mean they know how to communicate this knowledge to others and particularly to adults. Some pointers are given for consideration by anyone adopting this approach.

1. The trainer needs to establish an appropriate atmosphere and get acquainted with trainees prior to instruction, so that people are relaxed and effective communication can take place. To do this the trainer needs to: provide information about his or herself as well as about their role; discuss trainees' prior knowledge; establish what the trainee hopes to get out of the exercise; and positively encourage people to ask questions.

2. Adults require a degree of independence in learning. Scope should be provided for trainees to progress at their own pace.

3. Involvement in the training helps trainees

keep their brain active. This can be achieved by asking opinions about equipment.

4. Recognition should be given to trainees' prior experience which can be used to draw comparisons. This makes learning easier and shows respect for trainees' knowledge and established skills.

5. People should be able to see the benefits of what they are being taught, otherwise there will be resistance to learning.

6. Trainees should be given prompt opportunity to try out what they have learned, so that the information registers with them.

Staff selection

This section sets out to highlight the attributes that should be looked for in selecting staff to train as operators and supervisors or in recruiting staff. Although most organisations have screening tests for secretaries and typists, tests for word processing operators and supervisors are rare and still very much in the early stages of development. The following attributes are generally regarded as desirable for an *operator*.

1. A logical approach and problem solving ability to try out facilities, work through complex tasks and generally appreciate how the system (which is instructed by strictly logical command sequences) operates.

2. Practical, with an enjoyment of working with machines.

3. Ability to remain at a workstation for prolonged periods.

4. Low vulnerability to distraction – concentration is required when carrying out involved routines and steps that are irrecoverable.

5. Tidy and organised (to look after disc organisation, take care of other consumable items and cope with an involved work flow).

6. Creative ability (to experiment with features and facilities and find new applications).

7. Enjoyment of a challenge (to find new and

better ways of doing things and understand more of how the system works).

⑧ Good memory (to remember command sequences).

⑨ Ability to remain level-headed and coherent in fault situations (to interpret these and if necessary carry out specified diagnostic tests).

A *supervisor* should ideally be all of these things but also have the following attributes.

① Be good at communicating with people at all levels – operators, originators, management, other administrative staff, engineering and support people.

② Be good at selling the concepts of word processing.

③ Be sympathetic to people's needs, operators, originators and managers.

④ Be prepared to assume the role of operator in times of crisis or overload.

⑤ Be capable of devising, writing and implementing procedures.

⑥ Exhibit team leadership qualities.

⑦ Show an ability to set priorities.

⑧ Demonstrate planning and reporting skills.

The length of time taken to train staff depends on the system, their abilities, previous experience and it has been shown, their age. The tendency is for younger people to learn more rapidly although the ultimate level of knowledge and skills achieved seems independent of age. Those already accustomed to using VDU's also tend to acquire operating skills more quickly.

Checklist 11

The extent of new knowledge, understanding and skills required by staff is considerable.

Familiarisation:

☐ dispel common fears at an early stage;

☐ plan for orientation of originators and senior management;

☐ arrange seminars and visits;

☐ involve staff in equipment selection.

Operator and Supervisor Training:

☐ if purchasing a dedicated word processor you are likely to opt for what is offered by the supplier;

☐ formal training for word processing packages on micros is considerably more limited;

☐ independent training establishments can provide courses over an extended period of time;

☐ allow trainees time to practice and experiment;

☐ in-house training is a viable approach;

☐ scheduling formal training is critical;

☐ establishing a rapport with other sites can be a help.

Originator Training:

☐ originators need to understand and learn to adapt to new procedures and practices and to change previous habits;

☐ word processing does not mean originators can become sloppy in document preparation;

☐ encourage originators to learn at least the basics of how the system operates;

☐ management should be seen to be making use of the facilities.

Guidelines for In-house Trainers: assigning the role of trainer to someone who has not been trained to teach should not be taken lightly.

Staff Selection: a number of attributes have been identified as desirable for operators and supervisors.

PART IV

Costs and Contracts

Chapter 12 looks at the major cost areas of acquisition. Not just the cost of the system or of consumables needs to be accounted for, but maintenance, training, new furniture and paying for additional staff skills can be significant.

We recommended earlier that potential buyers get hold of suppliers' standard contracts and start negotiating. To expand on this we have included a chapter on contracts. Buyers usually find out too late that a contract to which they have paid little attention works to their disadvantage. We look at the areas for consideration within a contract when negotiating with a supplier.

Costs

The cost of ownership

So far we have discussed the different types of equipment available, the various approaches to handling basic word processing tasks, additional facilities that are increasingly being offered, as well as management and organisational issues relevant to supplier evaluation, equipment selection and installation. Chapter 12 consolidates the references made to cost factors throughout the preceding chapters and demonstrates the type of exercise that must be carried out in determining what it is all going to cost you. The outcome is that the price quoted by the salesman is only the tip of the iceberg!

No definitive prices can be given, and the significance of each cost element will vary tremendously from one situation to another. But we work through an example to emphasise the factors to be considered. At the end of the day, only you or someone appointed by you are in a position to calculate the figures for your organisation. Examples quoted are valid as at mid-1982, but remember that equipment costs are continuing to fall in real terms, whereas people costs will continue to rise. Printers will probably show the least cost reduction. The Japanese are now becoming a significant source of lower-priced printers after what was a US dominated market. But as printers are essentially electro-mechanical devices, developments that would result in dramatic price decreases are likely to be limited compared with processors, disc drives and VDU's.

Costing as practised by an accountant can take many forms – capital and revenue expenditure and life-cycle costing are two examples. Here we will use the concept of *total cost of ownership*, taking into account both external purchased goods and services and costs for formal staff training and back-up. In other words the cost of: equipment, software, consumables, ancillary equipment, furniture, installation and servicing, and operation.

Rent, lease or buy

The availability of tax allowances and your cash position will usually dictate this choice, if necessary your accountant will be able to advise. For those who are well versed in this area we suggest that you skip the following section and proceed with "Purchasing the System – Lock-in".

Purchase

Purchasing is simple and straightforward and you will normally be able to claim full capital allowance to offset against corporation tax. Alternatively you may wish to finance the purchase through hire-purchase arrangements (most suppliers offer this option and the major clearing banks can also provide hire purchase facilities). Once again full capital allowance can be claimed, although the initial outlay is much lower. Hire purchase agreements normally incorporate an interest charge of 6% or 7% above base rate.

Leasing

Leasing companies (again your supplier or bank can give introductions) purchase the equipment for you and then allow you the use of it for an agreed term. At expiry of the lease, payments are usually reduced to a nominal sum. Notionally leasing and hire purchase are very similar but the most significant difference lies in the tax allowances. With the former the leasing company claim the capital allowance and you can only offset the payments against corporation tax. For this reason leasing companies (who need the tax allowance now) usually work on a lower rate of interest than is offered with hire purchase.

Both leasing and hire purchase agreements present difficulties if you wish to sell the equipment before expiry of the agreement. Technically you do not own it and an arrangement must be negotiated with the finance company. Leases cannot incorporate a fixed-sum "buy-out" clause as this would effectively turn them into hire purchase agreements, thus jeopardising the tax advantages. The penalty for early termination is therefore difficult to assess and will almost certainly be unattractive. So, if you think there is a chance that you might want to sell the equipment on the second-hand market in the foreseeable future, it may be best to purchase outright, through overdraft finance if necessary.

Renting

Rental is usually the most expensive route, especially for agreements that allow termination after the first year. But this route does provide the greatest flexibility especially when the supplier is offering the rental direct. In this case he may be prepared to offer good terms for upgrades to newer equipment.

Most rental agreements run for much longer than originally envisaged and so-called "super-rentals" (the income after the original price has been paid off) provide the basis of many suppliers' finances.

Purchasing the system

Lock-in

Before we look at the details there is another factor of potentially greater consequence than the cost of ownership. It is what the manufacturers call "lock-in" and can be the reason behind their pricing policy on what are known as "entry-level" systems. Lock-in is the mechanism built into the marketing strategy that compels customer loyalty. Once you have purchased a system there is every reason to continue with the original supplier when a further system is needed. This is because discs have been created which only work with the supplier's equipment, staff have been trained and are now familiar with the system, good sources of consumable supplies have been found and investment made in bulk buying of these.

Changing manufacturer can cost at least as much again in intangibles as the purchase price of the system. Once committed, you are locked-in. Buying a system, using a bureau service for an initial period, or even being given a system on a free-trial basis may well lead you to an inevitable relationship with a supplier, effectively "forever". From the supplier's position every attempt will be made to make the initial purchase as attractive as possible to you. The entry-level system (the typical configuration for a new buyer) will be competitively priced and perhaps an initial trial period will be offered. The supplier knows that once you are committed, their future revenue is assured.

You must therefore look beyond the first step. However attractive the offer, examine the implications over something like a five-year period. Changing word processors is by no means as simple as selling a Ford Fiesta and buying a British Leyland Mini-Metro!

Initial Purchase Price of the System

Depending on what you require, initial purchase should cost between £4,000 and £10,000 per workstation. For the lowest price of a stand-alone dedicated system expect a slower daisywheel printer and lower capacity disc drives. For the top price expect a good mix of most of the features and facilities mentioned in this book, and the capability to extend the system with additional screens and printers. Communications facilities to allow a workstation to be linked to a computer or other workstations via a telephone line is also likely to be a working feature of systems at the top end of the market. The cost per workstation for a shared or distributed logic system tends to be about the same as its stand-alone equivalent. In general you get what you pay for, but three points may not be immediately obvious.

1. The cost of adding additional screens on some systems may be as much as the total price of other suppliers' systems.

2. The price of a microcomputer with word processing facilities tends to be at the lower end of the range.

3. Upgrading systems in a piece-meal fashion can be more expensive than acquiring a more comprehensive version from the outset.

Therefore, be clear about the price of enhancements and have a sound understanding of your true requirements for the immediate and foreseeable future. If you really need a variety of applications software as well as word processing, then a microcomputer rather than a dedicated word processor may be the best choice. If you have a regular word processing need with full-time keyboard staff, a purpose-designed word processor is probably what you should buy.

Extras and "Bundled" Prices

Some suppliers "bundle" extras within the purchase price. Others make the apparent price as low as possible and then charge separately for the extras. Points to account and watch for include:

1. Delivery (charge) – covers packaging, transport and handling.

2. Installation (charge) – covers setting up the machine in your office and getting it working.

3. Initial introduction (charge) – covers staff time in demonstrating the facilities after

delivery and installation and may be offered where the training provided is a self-teach package. This situation is particularly true if purchasing a microcomputer.

4. Software licence – software may be charged separately either as a one-off payment or as an annual or monthly fee, or a combination of both (i.e. an introductory payment plus recurring fee) and prices vary tremendously. Word processing packages to run on microcomputers can cost just a few hundred pounds. But this may entitle you only to the version current at the time. A new release may have to be paid for again in total if you want it. Software for shared or distributed logic systems may cost several thousand pounds.

5. Exchange rate variance – much equipment is imported, mainly from the US and increasingly from Japan. Some suppliers have the annoying habit of quoting a sterling price based on an old exchange rate which is then recalculated at purchase time. Be sure you know the rate used in sterling quotations. Like package holidays, the brochure price is not necessarily the market price.

6. Training courses cover course fees but not expenses for initial staff training. Those suppliers who "bundle" training into the purchase price usually provide initial training for one or perhaps two staff. Enquire about charges for additional training.

7. Warranty period – most suppliers give a warranty that the equipment is free from manufacturing defects. Some provide full maintenance cover for an initial period (which varies widely), others require that faulty equipment is returned to their depot for repair (which may take 1-2 weeks). Unless you plan to implement the system on a very relaxed timescale these latter warranties may be virtually worthless to you.

We will start by comparing the effect of these extras on two hypothetical systems. One is completely bundled at £6,000, the other with comparable facilities is priced at £5,000 but has hidden extras. The equipment comprises one workstation with processor (and internal memory), screen, keyboard, floppy disc drives and a daisywheel printer. In the case of the second system the exchange rate was originally quoted at $2.10 = £1, but at time of purchase the exchange rate is $1.95 = £1. The software licence is a one-off payment. Furthermore, although a three-month warranty period is offered for the second system, this entails delivering the equipment to the supplier's premises, the decision is therefore taken to start immediately with a maintenance contract at 20% of purchase price.

	£	£
Purchase price quoted	6,000	5,000
Delivery charge	incl.	incl.
Installation charge	incl.	250
Software licence	incl.	750
Exchange rate	Not applicable	385
Initial 3 days' course fees	incl.	300
3 months' full maintenance service	incl.	250
Price to purchase a working system	6,000	6,935
		(say £6,940)

As you will see our hidden extras system works out significantly more expensive.

This is a fairly stark example and a significant element, the exchange rate variance, has been known to operate in the other direction to the advantage of the customer. In reality only a few suppliers bundle as comprehensively as our example, but as is already clear, it is important to compare like with like when doing cost comparisons.

As "people" costs continue to rise it is likely that suppliers will continue to unbundle so that their ever increasing support staff costs can be covered through separate charges, giving the consumer the choice as to whether they wish to invest in these or not. Conversely, some suppliers persist with bundling as a deliberate selling feature.

Additional Costs of Installation

Before the equipment can be installed it may be necessary to have some extra sockets fitted, so that an electrician has to be hired. In addition a purpose-built table is required for the VDU and floppy-disc drives and for the printer. Most installations invest in a tractor-feed (with consequent additional stationery costs) or in a single-sheet feeder during their first year, if not at time of purchase. Let us

assume that we opt for a sheet-feeder. Likewise, an acoustic hood is quickly identified as a requirement.

The initial cost of installing the equipment therefore becomes:

	£	£
Total carried forward	6,000	6,940
Electrician	100	100
Tables (for VDU etc. & printer)	250	250
Sheet-feeder	750	750
Acoustic hood	350	350
Cost of installation	7,450	8,390

Operating costs

Consumables, maintenance, staff training and salary differentials all contribute to the operating costs and together have a significant impact on the cost of ownership.

Consumables

Consumption of print elements, ribbons, floppy discs, and stationery will depend on the throughput and organisation of the system, whether a tractor-feed or single-sheet feeder is used, the quality of consumables purchased, the quality of output expected, the scope for discounts through bulk purchasing, and how items are treated. As a rough estimate, for print elements, ribbons and floppy discs, you should budget for at least £600 p.a. and it could much more than this if dependent on the system supplier for these. Bear in mind that if increased productivity is expected from the system, then stationery and ribbon costs should increase relative to typewriter operations to reflect increased throughput. And special requirements such as mounted stationery may have to be allowed for.

Print Elements. Your usage of daisywheels (or thimbles) is such that the price differential between those that can be purchased from independent suppliers and those that must be purchased from the system supplier will not have a significant effect on budgeting for these. Remember, however, the points made in Chapter 8 about choice of typefaces and plastic versus metal wheels. Costs only begin to get significant where a large library of print elements is held, otherwise even plastic daisywheels will last for several months of continued usage. An organisation that tends to stick to one or two typestyles will not therefore be spending an enormous amount a year on these. However, it should still be taken into account even for these installations. We will suppose consumption averages out to a dozen daisywheels a year, and that we can use Diablo and Qume compatible wheels.

Ribbons. Printer ribbons are usually unique to each manufacturer's printer. Suppliers can therefore be expected to provide continuing supplies, but their most popularly installed printers have now attracted the attention of independent office supply companies. The competition that results has driven prices down and you may expect to pay about a third less for multi-supplier sourced ribbons than for those that must still be purchased from the system supplier. We mentioned in Chapter 8 that cloth ribbon is much cheaper and perfectly adequate for drafting but, in reality (as with typewriters) tends to be all too rarely used; assuming, therefore, that you use mainly multi-strike carbon ribbon, the annual cost of ribbon could well run to £400 – £500, or £600 and more for the less common printer types. This assumes a consumption of about 2 multi-strike carbon ribbons a week plus a cloth ribbon every couple of months. We will suppose that ribbons are readily available from a variety of suppliers for the models of printer in question.

Floppy Discs. Once again the competitive element introduced by independent suppliers has driven prices down. As with print elements, costs only begin to get significant as the library grows, for example at £3 each, a library of 60 discs means an investment of £180. Although the life expectancy of floppies is such that there is generally no need to replace well treated discs for a couple of years and only then if used extensively, discs will get damaged through maltreatment. Originators may also take their discs with them on moving jobs within a company. As new work is put on the system, work discs and archive and security copy discs get added to the library. So discs are an ongoing consumable item. It may take more than a year to build up a library of as many as 60, and although the number added in the second year of operation may not be as many as this, a typical installation could reasonably buy at least

another 30 during that and subsequent years. Where a system requires discs that must be formatted by the manufacturer costs are likely to be orders of magnitude more.

Stationery. Let us assume that we use 50 more sheets of letter-head a week, 50 more continuation and 100 more internal memo or rough draft. We will assume we do not have to arrange for any special stationery. We assume £20 per 1,000 for letter-head and continuation, £5 per 1,000 for the rest.

Let us return to our example. Allowing for the effect of consumables over 5 years:

	£	£
Total carried forward	7,450	8,390
Daisywheels (60 over 5 years)	360	360
Ribbons (550 over 5 years)	2,200	2,200
Floppy Discs (180 discs over 5 years)	540	540
Additional Stationery	650	650
TOTAL	11,200	12,140

Strictly speaking purchases made into the future should be discounted to allow for the use of the money up to the point of purchase, but we shall ignore this for the purposes of our example.

Maintenance

Once the initial warranty period has expired a decision must be taken about future maintenance. Unfortunately, although equipment costs have come down dramatically and most systems are fairly reliable the cost of keeping a fleet of maintenance engineers continues to rise. Over a five-year period maintenance may well cost as much as initial purchase – by the end of the 1980's it will probably cost very much more.

As we indicated in Chapter 7, suppliers may offer a range of maintenance services with prices geared to the response required. Typical options are:

☐ "A" level – an engineer will call within 24 hours of a reported breakdown;

☐ "B" level – an engineer will call within 3 days of a reported breakdown;

☐ "C" level – an engineer will call when available.

The A-level service can cost 20% of the purchase price per annum, C-level may be only 12%. In practice few users can tolerate the delays that B and C-levels imply. In the nature of things a fault is only manifest when you are using or wanting to use the system. As often as not you need the output then, not in two or three days time.

Suppliers usually offer two time-and-parts alternatives. The first is "call-out". An engineer visits your installation and repairs the system. An hourly charge (about £30) is made for their time and any spare parts needed are added to the bill. Response is usually on the come-when-they-can basis and there is often a hefty call-out charge (a £70 fee is not unknown) to encourage users to enter a formal maintenance contract. The second is "return to workshop". You deliver the faulty equipment back to the contractor or supplier's workshop and collect it when ready. This avoids the call-out fee and usually the hourly rate is lower.

An option mentioned in Chapter 7 is to avoid a formal maintenance contract altogether and to buy a second machine. When a breakdown occurs the second system is used and the first one is repaired on a time-and-parts basis. Purchasing a second system just in case there is a breakdown sounds dramatic. In fact maintenance costs make this option well worth considering for users who already have two or three working systems. Even the one-system user may find the additional cost over the A-level maintenance justified by the immediate availability of a stand-by, which presumably will not remain idle in the meantime.

In our worked example, we include maintenance figures for 4¾ years A-level service at 20% of initial purchase price. Remember, the first three months was allowed for when calculating the price to purchase a working system.

Training

Training costs are incurred in two stages. First there is the obvious cost of courses, not to mention expenses (and perhaps employing agency staff to cover during the course). Second there is the cost in lost efficiency while staff become familiar with the system. After the basic formal training, a possible advanced facilities session of a day or so two months later may be desirable. Unfortunately no-one can be certain of continuing staff

loyalty and some budgetary allowance should be made for training new staff during the life of the equipment. In our example we assume the suppliers include in the price an initial training course for one operator. We decide to invest in an additional three-day course for a second operator and assume a three-day course is needed roughly every two years to train new staff. Finally, we send all staff involved on an advanced 2-day training course a few months after their initial training.

Agency Staff

In looking at your workload profile and considering the benefits of word processing, you may estimate that investment in a system will mean you no longer need to use agency staff for overload situations. However, you may still have to employ such staff to cater for annual leave situations and someone with relevant word processing experience will be required. Word processing "temps" cost a little more than "temp" secretaries/typists but the real difficulty arises when trying to find one at short notice who knows your particular system. By now you should appreciate that a word processor is not like a typewriter – it needs special training to be used effectively and its workload must be organised properly if maximum benefit is to be derived from it. It is therefore worth enquiring about the availability of suitably skilled agency staff before buying a system – this can be especially true of some of the less well-known and difficult systems to learn.

Turning once again to our costing example let us look at the impact of those running costs. We assume that the cost of a word processing "temp" is £50 per week more than for an ordinary typist "temp". Again for simplicity, we have not discounted annual payment, but the overall picture is more important than the detailed figures.

	£	£
TOTAL Carried Forward	11,200	12,140
Maintenance	5,700	4,750
Initial training 2nd operator	300	300
New staff training over 5 years	600	600
8 days advanced training/5 years	800	800
Additional cost of temps (3 wks. p.a.)	750	750
TOTAL	19,350	19,340

The cost of the two systems now begins to look comparable and we need carry forward just one total.

Perhaps these figures seem frightening when compared with the initial price of £5,000 and £6,000. But remember we have yet to include the biggest cost of all – the cost of permanent staff.

Permanent Staff

Increasing efficiency by word processing should be compared with the cost of operating with conventional typewriters. These too have some maintenance costs, use ribbon and must be purchased, leased or rented. Finally, to make our comparison complete, we shall allow for the fact that permanent staff with word processing skills can probably demand higher salaries than those with only typing skills. Our last set of figures therefore includes a typing alternative. We have assumed the annual salary of a skilled word processing operator is £1,000 more than for a typist. It is usually accepted that office staff cost about twice their annual salary when overheads are taken into account; so we also need to take into account the additional overheads. Our typewriter is assumed to cost £600 with an annual maintenance bill of £100 and consumables consumption of £200 a year.

	£	£
TOTAL carried forward		19,350
Typewriter & consumables/5 years	2,100	
Salary difference/5 years		5,000
Overheads difference/5 years		5,000
TOTAL	2,100	29,350
Difference		27,250

If we assume the annual salary and overheads for a typist are each £6,000, then the total cost of employing a typist over the five years together with typewriter and consumables is about £62,000. The figure for a word processing operator with equipment and consumables is around £90,000.

Conclusions

Our illustration figures have been used to give you a "feel" for the cost of word processing. Hopefully, you will be encouraged to work out your own detailed costings before making a decision. However, let us try to draw some conclusions from our guideline figures:

1. Word processing can cost almost half as much again as conventional typing. Its *benefits in terms of efficiency and effectiveness* therefore need to be at or better than this level.

2. The cost of the equipment is probably the least important item. Additional benefits derived from *more and better facilities suited to your needs are almost certainly worth paying for.* For similar reasons, second-hand equipment does not really represent a significant saving. But it might be viable for a one-man business or for a stand-buy.

3. Buying a word processor is a significant decision. *It should be evaluated very carefully.*

Checklist 12

The cost of the equipment is only a fraction of the overall costs involved. The total cost of ownership is what is important.

Rent, lease, or buy are all viable approaches.

Purchasing the system:

☐ be aware of getting "locked-in" to a supplier;

☐ take account of extras such as delivery and installation charges, software licence, exchange rate variance, and training courses;

☐ allow for additional costs of installation such as site preparation, furniture, and ancillary equipment;

☐ budget for consumables, maintenance, on-going training, and salary differentials.

Simple price comparisons are misleading. In fact, purchase price is probably the least important item.

Contracts

Why have a contract?

What to look for in a contract

Can the terms be negotiated?

Checklist

13

The purchase of a word processing system is invariably covered by a contract drawn up by the supplier. Surprisingly few purchasers take the trouble to look at the terms in detail and even fewer take proper legal advice. Yet computer companies have acquired a reputation for accepting very little contractual responsibility and a regrettably high proportion of buyers later find that the contract conditions work to their disadvantage. This short chapter aims to cover the main points to be examined but cannot be regarded as a substitute for proper advice.

Why have a contract?

Contracts act to clarify the relationship between buyer and seller. In the event of a *dispute* it is the contract that should specify the responsibilities of each party. In a normal happy relationship the contract merely gathers dust, but when things go wrong it is comforting to know that there is a point of reference that can be enforced, by law if necessary. Contracts therefore tend to take the black view of things, they exist for black circumstances!

In the UK considerable legislation exists about the sale of goods and the protection of buyers against unscrupulous vendors. This legislation and the result of past cases comprises what is known as "common law". In the absence of a definitive contract common law takes over and even when there is such a contract some of the terms may be invalidated by laws (such as the Unfair Contract Terms Act) which have been enacted to protect consumers.

Common law is not usually adequate for complex equipment such as word processors. Firstly, it does not cope fully with the problems that can occur and secondly it places burdens on the supplier which he may be anxious to avoid. It is this second reason that is important to you. Since the supplier usually draws up the contract, you may be sure that he is more concerned about protecting himself against liabilities than he is in guarding your interests in a possible case against him.

What to look for in a contract

The details of a contract for word processing equipment usually run to several pages. There are a number of areas to watch for.

Specification. Is there a clear specification of the equipment, or does it just refer to an "XYZ word processor"? Some features may have been mentioned by the salesman, some may have been demonstrated, but at contract time they should all be spelt out in detail. It is no good discovering later that the features you thought you were buying are not on your equipment if the contract only refers to an XYZ model and leaves it in the supplier's hands to say what an XYZ model is.

Acceptance. Complex equipment is always prone to failure and electronic equipment has a tendency to be especially vulnerable on first arrival. Fortunately, this is the time when the customer holds the whip-hand. Unless you have paid in full before delivery (an unusual occurrence), you still have the money. It is therefore wise to run an "acceptance test" to put the machine through its paces before accepting the equipment. This test, which you should devise at the time of contract should ideally test out all the equipment and may take half-a-day to complete. You want to ensure at least that the screen maintains a steady flicker-free image, that the printer quality and speed match up to the specification particularly after an hour or more's pounding, and that the disc drives are in good working order.

Acceptance testing gives you the opportunity to get things put right which otherwise may never be fixed. Obviously outright failures (so-called "dead-on arrival") are easy to observe, but factors such as the quality of printing are very subjective. Once the machine has been paid for it can be difficult to persuade the supplier that these "grey areas" are his responsibility. Do not be shy on insisting that the acceptance test is fully met before you make any payment. It is your best chance to establish the correct relationship with the supplier and his engineering maintenance staff.

Payment. The contract will certainly specify when payment is to be made. Sometimes there will be a deposit on order, usually final payment is due on delivery (or acceptance).

Maintenance Life. Suppliers are often reticent to state the maintenance life of the equipment or indeed to guarantee the continuing existence of a maintenance service. What you should ask for is a contractual commitment that maintenance and spares will be available for at least five years.

Exclusions. Be especially on guard for clauses that exclude all statements that may have been made by the salesman. Suppliers find it impossible to be certain that their salesmen never exaggerate or make inaccurate claims and this form of exclusion may attempt to invalidate the very promises that made you decide on this supplier (the Unfair Contract Terms Act and other laws may still be of some comfort). Where exclusions exist make sure that the specification includes all the points that were vital to you in making your choice and that these are expressed clearly and unambiguously.

Can the terms be negotiated?

Salesmen can be nervous about contracts. They often do not fully understand them. Because of the black circumstances that they are designed to meet, salesmen do not find "Terms and Conditions" fit well with their customary motivation and enthusiasm. Customers who wish to negotiate contracts are especially unpopular. It means the salesman will have to fight within his company's management structure to gain acceptance of the customer's point-of-view.

Do not be put off by this reticence but do be sure that:

☐ your negotiations occur at the right time; and

☐ your requests are reasonable.

The right time is **not** when you have decided which machine to buy. At this stage you have made your mind up, possibly taken on commitments such as promises to train staff, and are eager to get on with it. Under these conditions you will almost certainly settle for second-best.

Ask for a copy of the contract as soon as you are happy that the supplier has a possibility of meeting your needs. Examine it and others well before you make your final choice and raise any objections in plenty of time. This way you will choose the machine together with its conditions of supply. You may be able to get changes to those conditions as an inducement to make you decide on a particular supplier.

Lastly, you may have found this section a little depressing. But not all suppliers are rogues and not all salesmen dishonest. These are the exception, not the rule.

Checklist 13

In the event of a dispute the contract should specify the responsibilities of each party.

Areas to consider are:

☐ the system specification;

☐ an acceptance test;

☐ when payment is to be made;

☐ commitment to a specified maintenance life;

☐ exclusions.

Negotiate before finalising the supplier.

Epilogue

In this section we take a brief look at likely developments in word processing equipment together with developments that are contributing towards the convergence of equipment towards the "automated office". And finally, we conclude with a summary of important points we would like you to bear in mind.

Developments in Word Processors

There are a number of developments in word processing equipment anticipated by those involved in the industry and likely to occur over the next few years.

1. Developments in screen technology that will result in:

    ☐ full-page display becoming common with even larger displays also more widely available;

    ☐ the ability to view separate sections from the same or different documents at the same time;

    ☐ higher resolution screens with improved quality in character display and legibility;

    ☐ greater graphics capability and ability to display non-standard characters;

    ☐ multi-colour displays;

    ☐ multi-use terminals – for word processing, viewdata, management workstations and as computer terminals.

2. Improved designs of keyboard for faster keying speed and greater operator comfort.

3. Higher capacity, more robust floppy disc storage and smaller, more compact hard disc storage devices.

4. Printers will still be around to produce permanent easily readable records. Developments will include faster, quieter and more reliable single-element printers, improved quality dot matrix printers, and more reliable, cheaper ink-jet printers.

5. Increased internal memory for relatively little extra cost.

6 New designs and improved reliability of single-sheet feeders.

7 Enhanced information processing facilities (for searching, sorting, record processing) interfaced to word processing software.

8 A wider range of communications facilities to other equipment.

9 Integration of voice facilities for recording messages.

Your Next Stage

Most organisations investing in their first word processor should probably allow at least two years to acquire experience and confidence in using the equipment, coupled with adaptation to new disciplines and organisational changes required. Then they can seriously contemplate the next major stage in office automation. But before doing so it will be important to evaluate the success of the investment to date. Evaluation should cover tangible and intangible benefits and in particular performance with respect to:

☐ the equipment;

☐ throughput; and

☐ the organisation (measured in terms of the organisation's functions and objectives).

Equipment performance can be assessed on the basis of speed of operation, capabilities, and reliability (including the efficiency of the supplier's support services). Throughput performance will depend on: the equipment; the attitudes, morale, and interactions of the personnel involved (operators, originators, and management responsible); the procedures adopted; and the flexibility and scope for individual initiative. Finally, organisational performance will depend on all of these together with control over the workflow, adaptability to new methods and appreciation of the application areas.

Assessing these aspects of performance should identify further areas for improvements in the running of the office. Part of any word processing sales pitch is usually to claim that once typed, an item of correct text need never be typed again. But this is only true within the confines of the office preparing the document in question. The text may already have been typed by an external body if not another department within the same company. Does the originator of the moment know whether material is being rekeyed once the document has been distributed? We suggested in Chapter 2 that any investigation of requirements should also include a look at the before and after stages of documents being prepared.

Elimination of any unnecessary rekeying before origination or after distribution could well be your next stage in office automation. However, this will very much depend on provision of the necessary interfaces and it is in this area that some of the major developments will take place.

WP/DP Interfaces

Here we are talking about interfacing data processing files and word processing files, whether on the same machine or between a computer and a dedicated word processor or micro running a word processing package. Data processing files tend to be tightly structured, strictly coded, content significant, and the information is usually quantitative. Word processing files are just the opposite, with any interface having to take care of the random appearance of control characters as well as coping with upper and lower case.

Interfaces will increasingly be offered by suppliers in the form of conversion software to allow information to be extracted from data processing files and converted to a word processing file. Nonetheless, the user still has to specify exactly what has to be extracted and how it should be reformatted. This could involve tailor-made additional software. Generally, however, the aim of suppliers developing such facilities is to allow the user to specify requirements as a set of parameters that the software will take care of. Typical application areas are credit control letters, selective mail-shots to clients, personnel correspondence, and accountancy summaries, all based on information extracted from a company's computer files.

Conversely, some users generate the original information on their word processor and require this or relevant parts to be transferred to a computer file for further processing. (It is also feasible that a user will want to store word processing files on a larger computer for archive purposes and this should be a standard feature in any distributed logic system). In that case special software has to be written since something that is loosely structured must be converted to a tightly structured entity. Typical application areas are the creation of corporate filing systems and indexing of textual databases.

Interfaces to Other Electronic Equipment

Equipment such as photocopiers, facsimile transmission devices, phototypesetters and telephone systems are now being electronically controlled, with the consequence that links are becoming increasingly feasible between the different items as well as with word processors. As we mentioned in Chapter 6, these depend on interfaces to physically connect the hardware whether directly via the telephone line, or by some other communication channel. They also depend on software which allows the information stored in a form meaningful to one piece of equipment to be translated into that understood by another, and caters for however many communication channels and physical interfaces are involved in-between.

Limited facilities are already available and will continue to develop, particularly in the following areas.

Word processor to:

☐ word processor

☐ computer

☐ telex tape cutter or directly into the telex network

☐ magnetic storage device interfaced to an electric typewriter

☐ intelligent copier or printer

☐ facsimile device

☐ phototypesetter

☐ optical character recognition (OCR) equipment.

Communication Channels

There is an increasing demand for full communication between word processors (irrespective of supplier and model) and between word processors and other terminals to provide more efficient and effective means of exchanging information. Communication channels can involve:

☐ a network of leased lines (private wires);

☐ the public switched telephone network (PSTN);

☐ the packet switched service (PSS) for high speed data transmission;

☐ the telex network;

☐ radio transmission;

☐ satellite;

☐ microwave links;

☐ a local area network.

Local area networks are intended to link equipment around the office (along corridors and between floors). A number of basic designs are being developed but the two best known are Ethernet and the Cambridge Ring. Some suppliers are adapting these, yet others are developing totally different approaches. Some will only link the suppliers own equipment (classed as "closed" networks), others offer interconnection of a heterogeneous range of devices ("open" networks).

A system called Teletex is being developed that may significantly contribute towards satisfying the needs for improved means of information exchange demanded by the business community. It is based on the idea of using the existing public switched telephone network, the packet switched service and the telex network. The intention is to provide a basis for national and international text communication. All terminals connected to the teletex network will have to meet certain minimum specifications.

At the same time developments are taking place with the voice network for transmission of data, text and facsimile messages at higher data rates and capacities than previously available.

The Executive Workstation

Secretarial and clerical costs make up only a small proportion of office costs when compared with the costs of executives, so that a small increase in executive productivity can be worth more than a significantly greater increase in typing efficiency. Efforts are being concentrated, therefore, on improving the effectiveness and efficiency of the executive. The result is that the executive or managerial workstation concept has been introduced.

These are being based on word processor terminal design and operation but with the following aids:

- diary facilities;

- voice integration;

- access to information from personal and "public" (i.e. company) files;

- a pad for written input.

Managerial workstations will be linked into a network of workstations including those operated by secretarial staff.

So You Want to Buy a Word Processor?

With the number and variety of systems currently on the market, no text of this nature can hope to be totally comprehensive in covering the different approaches to how these carry out their word processing tasks. What we have aimed to do is to categorise the major areas for evaluation, describe the relevant features and facilities, and to summarise the pros and cons of different approaches. The objective is to provide a solid framework from which you can specify requirements and assess what suppliers have to offer. In addition we have covered matters that will ease the introduction of equipment into the office and help you get the most out of it. To conclude:

1. Do devote time and effort to analysing your situation and specifying requirements.

2. Pay serious attention to the managerial and organisational issues, devote time to the "people" aspects, and thoroughly involve staff from "Day One".

3. In evaluating equipment:

    - do not be fobbed off with slick sales talk;

    - watch how your sample workload is dealt with;

    - allow potential operators to try out equipment;

    - ensure that special requirements are thoroughly demonstrated;

    - ask existing users if they would buy the same equipment next time.

4. It is unlikely that you will find a system that perfectly matches your requirements. Aim for the best compromise, but better a compromise based on a well-integrated design with a few weak areas rather than a mediocre offering of all facilities.

5. Work on the basis of total cost of ownership.

6. Opting for a word processing package on a general purpose micro offers scope for a multi-function system, but its use as a word processor will not be in the same class as a system dedicated to the job.

7. Be prepared for initial teething troubles.

8. Unless prepared to invest heavily in helping suppliers develop the convergence of office equipment, steer clear of communication and interfacing technology until you have come to grips with word processing applications.

9. A word processor is not an end in itself capable of understanding and initiative, but merely a tool, the value of which lies in its ability to do the job and the proficiency of the people using it. And that goes for originators as well as operators.

And finally, we wish you success. Success that will lead to:

- greater productivity and effectiveness from originators and typists;

- improved standards of presentation;

- a smoother workload with unavoidable peaks far easier to cope with; and

- increased job satisfaction for all involved.

Appendix 1

Sources of further information

No doubt some of the addresses, telephone numbers and points of contact will change during the life of the book. But we believe it is helpful to include them since many will remain static and for those that do change, at least you will have a starting point from which you can be referred further. The list is not intended to be exhaustive.

Supplier Information

The following are useful for information (some in the form of advertisements) about suppliers of word processing systems, consumables, ancillary equipment and furniture, as well as word processing bureaux, consultancies, or training facilities and establishments.

Datapro Reports on Word Processing. A loose-leaf information service including reviews of systems, updated on a monthly basis, SFrs. 1,435. Datapro Research Corporation, CH-1164 Buchillon, Switzerland, telephone 76 37 31. The publication should be available in a few large reference libraries and in particular the Science Reference Library, Southampton Buildings, 25 Chancery Lane, London WC2, telephone 01 405 8721.

Guide to Word Processing Systems. Provides details in tabular form for comparison of features and facilities of systems, includes training available, consumable suppliers and consultancies. Published annually at £24. ECC Publications, 30-31 Islington Green, London N1 8BJ, telephone 01 359 7481.

Personal Computer World. Provides reviews of microcomputer applications packages including word processing. Published by Sportscene Publishers (PCW) Ltd., 14 Rathbone Place, London W1P 1DE, telephone 01 631 1433.

Which Computer? (monthly) and the supplement *Which Word Processor?* (quarterly). The latter provides reviews of equipment in each issue, regular listings of suppliers and bureaux, as well as ad hoc articles of interest to word processor users. Which Computer? provides reviews of microcomputer applications packages including word processing.

Published by ECC Publications, 30-31 Islington Green, London N1 8BJ, telephone 01 359 7481.

Ergonomics and "People" Issues

APEX. Published "The New Technology Health and Safety Guidelines", price 50p. Address: Head Office, 22 Worple Road, London SW19, telephone 01 947 3131.

The Association of Optical Practitioners Ltd. Published "VDU's and You – Information for Operators", free-of-charge and "Vision and VDU's", price £1.75. Address: Bridge House, 233-234 Blackfriars Road, London SE1 8NW, telephone 01 261 9661.

ASTMS. Published "Guide to Health Hazards of VDU's", 50p to members, £2 to non-members. Address: 10 Jamestown Road, London NW1, telephone 01 267 4422.

AUEW (TASS). Published "Health Hazards of VDU's", free-of-charge. Address: Onslow Hall, Little Green, Richmond, Surrey, telephone 01 948 2271.

Butler Cox and Partners Ltd. Published "Eyetests and VDU Users", the final report of the VET (VDU Eye Test) Advisory Group, free-of-charge. Address: 26 Holborn Viaduct, London EC1A, telephone 01 583 9381.

The Equal Opportunities Commission. Published "Information Technology in the Office: The Impact on Women's Jobs", 1980, carried out by Communications Studies and Planning Ltd., free-of-charge. Address: Overseas House, Quay Street, Manchester M3 5HW, telephone 061 833 9244.

HUSAT Research Group, Department of Human Sciences, Loughborough University of Technology. Extensive work has been done by the group on the human aspects of advanced technology and a number of papers have been published. Their address is The Elms, Elms Grove, Loughborough, Leicestershire LE11 1RG.

IFRA – Inca Fieg Research Association (International Research Association for Newspaper Technology): a German based organisation, who published "The VDT Manual" by A Cakir, D J Hart, J F M Stewart. The HUSAT Group were involved in this work together with the Technical University of Berlin. Their address is IFRA, Washingtonplatz 1, D-6100 Darmstadt, Federal Republic of Germany. This publication should be available through library channels.

Manpower Services Commission. Published the findings of a study into the training needs and provisions amongst companies using text processing technology, carried out by Research Bureau Ltd., 1982. Address: Training Services Division, Room W449, Moorfoot, Sheffield S1 4PQ, telephone 0742 753275.

Associations and Membership Organisations

These groups have been established to promote the exchange of ideas, views and experiences and in some cases to enhance professional status. They may hold meetings, arrange seminars and conferences, publish newsletters, journals, reports and occasional papers, as well as offer assistance and carry out surveys of their membership.

British Computer Society Word Processing and Office Automation Group, annual subscription £5. Contact Les Wright, Treasurer, c/o British Gas Corporation, National Westminster House, 326 High Holborn, London WC1, telephone 01 242 0789.

Institute of Word Processing was founded in 1982 to establish standards and professional qualifications in the field. Address: 173-175 Cleveland Street, London W1, telephone 01 380 0388, 01 836 6767/6467.

International Information/Word Processing Association, annual subscription £25. Address: 1015 N. York Road, Willow Grove, PA 1090 or the UK representative is Norah Barckley, 161 Studland Road, London W7, telephone 01 578 4130.

The Office Automation Network is an association of independent consultants and consulting firms expert in the application of computing and communications systems to the work of commercial, administrative and educational organisations. Contact Roger Whitehead at Office Futures, 14 Amy Road, Oxted, Surrey RH8 0PX, telephone (via) 01 404 5011.

OFIX (Office of the Future Information Exchange) is a user group aimed at the small to medium size organisation approaching and in the early stages of office automation. Contact the Chairman, Graham Wise, c/o Mazda Cars (UK) Ltd., Longfield Road, Tunbridge Wells, Kent TN2 3EY, telephone 0892 40123.

Trade Associations and Professional Bodies. Many of these have formed their own special interest group in word processing and office automation. Readers' own trade associations or professional institutes may have done so.

Exhibitions

IBS, International Business Show, arranged by the Business Equipment Trade Association (BETA), 8 Southampton Place, London WC1A 2EF, telephone 01 405 6233. Held annually in the autumn.

Information Technology and Management Exhibition (abbreviated Info '83, '84, etc.), arranged by BED Exhibitions Ltd., 44 Wallington Square, Wallington, Surrey SM6 8RG, telephone 01 647 1001. Held annually early in the year in London.

International Word Processing Exhibition, arranged by the Business Equipment Trade Association (BETA), 8 Southampton Place, London WC1A 2EF, telephone 01 405 6233. Held annually in the spring in London.

The Which Computer? Show, sponsored by the publishers of Which Computer? (see the entry under "Supplier Information"). Held annually at the beginning of the year in London.

Miscellaneous

Proof-correction marks British Standard BS5261 covers copy preparation and proof correction. The standard has been established for the publishing and printing industries. It includes recommended marks for copy preparation and proof correction that can also be used in the normal office. The standard is published in two parts but all that is needed is a separately published fold-out card with extracts from Part 2 and entitled "Marks for Copy Preparation and Proof Correction", reference number BS 5261C. This can be purchased for £2.60 from the BSI Sales Department, 101 Pentonville Road, London N1, telephone 01 837 8801.

Appendix 2
Detailed recommendations for system operation

This Appendix is a supplement to Chapter 10.

Disc library

Disc Organisation

Methods used to organise floppy disc libraries vary from one installation to another and depend on the type of work being done, the number and type of staff involved, and the size of the library. For an organisation where work or staff are likely to be shared across a number of word processing systems, it will be less confusing if the same approach to disc and document organisation is used throughout. The points made about floppy disc organisation can be applied to the partitioning of a hard disc. The following approaches are common.

1. Each originator has a disc or set of discs for their work.

2. Discs are allocated to specific sets of documents in a publication series (some documents such as manuals or lengthy reports may take up a whole disc or more to themselves).

3. Disc allocation is based on the subject matter of the documents (for example, general staff matters, a client or set of clients, product areas).

It may be that a combination of approaches is required. There are a number of points for those responsible for a floppy disc library to bear in mind when devising a system.

1. Where standard formats or text are used extensively, it may be convenient to copy these to all relevant work discs when discs are first formatted.

2. The need to change over data discs during a session should be kept to a minimum and is dependent on the organisation of documents across discs and how the workload is likely to be organised throughout each day.

3. Some originators may prefer to take their discs away from the word processor.

4. In a shared typing service with more than one workstation, originators may have a variety of work on different documents carried out simultaneously by more than one operator. They will therefore require a series of discs for their work.

5. With long documents it may be better to allocate them a floppy to themselves rather than running out of disc space on a partly used disc, particularly when the document could be lengthened on a subsequent draft.

6. Where a variety of standard format documents are used for different types of work held on different discs throughout the library, it may be convenient to hold the format documents on a master disc of their own ready to be copied across to new discs as needed. Examples are: memo, letter, and telex formats; standard headers and footers; and standard lists of addressees – for merging in as a distribution list on correspondence or reports.

7. For security reasons, some discs may need to be kept under lock and key, especially overnight, or disc passwords if available may be used. Disc organisation that allows the number of these to be kept to a minimum will probably prove more convenient.

8. Once a document is completed it may need to be retained but it may be some time before it will be worked on again. If this is a common occurrence, an archive or set of archive discs could be established to allow such documents to be copied (dumped) thus freeing space on work discs.

9. If a number of people use the system, organisation of the disc library should be self-explanatory and easy to follow.

Disc Naming and Filing

Some installations reference discs by giving them a number in a strict sequence, others use something more meaningful. If the former approach is used then the discs are stored in numeric sequence. But a cross-reference for contents will be needed to help an operator to decide on which disc a new piece of work should be put, and to cater for those times when a document is returned for correction or update without a note of its disc reference.

If discs are given a meaningful name or code they can be filed alphanumerically by name. In systems that require the disc name to be specified to access a document on it, names should be kept short for operator convenience.

Where security copies of discs are held, some standard and easily recognisable means of naming these should be devised – even if only preceding or ending all names with for example S, SE, or SEC. All such security copies should be clearly marked to avoid confusion with the master copy.

Document logging

Similar comments apply in respect of document reference. (Note a few systems may force the operator to allocate a reference devised by the system but it is more common for the operator to have to allocate a name for each document created.) A numbering system may be appropriate for your organisation, in which case it is vital that a record is kept of what each document is about. Or a number reference may be appropriate in some instances and not others. For example the chapters of a book or major report (to which a floppy or set of floppies is devoted) may be held as separate documents referred to by chapter number. Operators and originators, however, generally prefer to *give documents names that are more meaningful*. The important point about this approach is to try and keep the names as short as possible for operator convenience in accessing documents.

One of the most disciplinary requirements in maintaining a disc library, however, is to *devise and maintain a system for quick identification* of where a previously typed document is held in the library. This may involve maintaining printed indexes for all discs listing the documents they hold. These indexes can usually be generated automatically by the system. But such printed records must be kept totally up-to-date by operators, even if it means marking them up by hand until sufficiently messy to warrant printing off a fresh copy. This approach may be adequate if it is obvious that the document will be limited to one or two possible discs (an operator does

not want to scan through every disc index to find where a document is located). Or the work may be sufficiently consistent and the disc library organised in such a way that the location of any document is obvious, in which case it may be acceptable not to maintain printed copies of disc indexes but to refer to these on the screen. Such situations are unlikely once a library grows to any size.

Where the type of work is varied and particularly where a number of originators are involved, a method for recording the disc and document name reference, either on the document or on an accompanying form is likely to be necessary. If a *form* is used, then it can also provide a means for the originator to record information that will help the operator in first setting up a document and each time they come to edit and print it (such as headings/footings to be used, typestyle(s), and paper requirements). If the originator has not been specific about these, the operator can add the necessary details to the form based on their own decisions about format and lay-out.

Most word processing systems provide a means whereby these formatting details are recorded with the document on the disc for reference purposes. Nonetheless, a form is still a good idea as it can remain with the printed document at all times until the document is deleted from the disc. In this way it provides the disc and document name reference whenever a draft is submitted for further editing, or the document is retrieved from a paper filing system and submitted for update. If and when a document is no longer required to be held on disc, the originator can mark it accordingly and submit it to the operator with the request to delete the document. The form can then be destroyed.

The following headings are worth considering if the form approach is to be adopted – they do not all have to be included, nor completed each time; they should serve merely as prompts when appropriate:

Originator/Location/Tele. Ext.

Operator

Date Required (could be for next draft or final copy)

Disc Name (completed by the originator if they have a preference as to where it is stored)

Document Name (completed by the originator if they have a preference)

Brief Description

Expiry Date (some systems allow an expiry date to be set before which time an operator will not be allowed to delete the document)

Security Copy Required (the work is sufficiently involved or important that a complete copy needs to be held on another disc)

Confidentiality Level (may need to be locked away, or require a document password)

Header/Footer Details (all pages to be marked COMPANY RESTRICTED, all pages to be numbered at the foot in the centre e.g. "Page x", etc.)

Typestyle (Prestige Elite, Courier 10, etc.)

Lay-out/Printing Instructions (left-hand margin of 6, right-hand justification, drafts in one-and-half spacing, letter-headed paper, number of carbon copies, cloth or carbon ribbon, envelope also required, etc.)

Request to Delete (could be signified by a tick or a signature)

Request to Archive (could be signified by a tick or a signature)

Progress Details (if several operators are likely to work serially on a document, it may help to have space to record how far each one has reached so that the next person to pick up the work knows exactly where the previous operator left off. Where a number of operators are servicing a number of originators, it may be sensible to provide room for recording the date the work was received and the date the work began.)

It is pointless to store documents that are no longer used – both originators and operators should be encouraged to keep their discs in a *"tidy"* state. It may be that presenting originators with a list of their documents once-a-month will encourage them in this activity.

In situations where originators occasionally do their own document preparation, they may prove less disciplined in logging document details, and need to be actively encouraged to do so.

Maintenance
Hardware
Keeping equipment clean. Although the equipment is resilient it must be kept clean – a routine can be established for regularly dusting down the system, and in particular wiping the video screens. With the same end in mind, eating and smoking over and around equipment ought to be discouraged. Anyone cleaning the word processor needs to be aware of recommended procedures and the fact that solvents may damage the video screens or casing. Purpose made cleaning wipes for VDU's are available from a variety of suppliers.

Disc Drives. Cleaning kits are available for floppy disc drives and the recommendation by their suppliers is that they be used on drives every two to four weeks. These products have been introduced for the micro-computer market. The kit uses a vinyl sleeve (the same as those enclosing the standard floppy) with a piece of material inserted in it (where the floppy normally is) that can be soaked with cleaning fluid, or alternatively a fresh cleaning disc is inserted into the sleeve for each cleaning operation. If the system is in a very dusty or smoky environment or there is no regular maintenance carried out on it, then it is certainly advisable to invest in one of these. In this way the disc heads are kept clean as a safeguard against disc corruption, as well as to maintain the drives in good working order, but check with your system supplier or maintenance contractor first.

Engineer Call-out. Whenever maintenance engineers are called-out, record the visit for later reference should the fault recur. Certainly any problem leading to call-out of engineers should be logged to help in fault diagnosis.

Printer. Pens, pencils, paper clips or similar items should not be placed on the printer in case these fall into the works. Check with the supplier or engineers about cleaners that are suitable for the platen.

Acoustic Screen. If you have one of these, the

window should be kept clean and care taken against scratching.

Consumables

Print Elements. Leaving daisywheels and thimbles lying around exposes them to potential damage and loss. Special compact binders are now being supplied to store these, but each element comes in its own protective case and these are perfectly adequate for prolonged storage and use, provided a suitable container or drawer is found to file them in. Just like typewriter heads, print elements can get clogged with printer ribbon residue through prolonged use. Cleaning brushes and special cleaning ribbons are available to clean typestyles.

Ribbons. Similarly, partly-used ribbon cartridges left lying around can easily get damaged – the exposed ribbon may get crinkled and has to be wound on further, or if it snaps, the cartridges becomes useless. Carbon ribbons are especially vulnerable in this way.

Floppy Discs. Your supplier will no doubt include guidelines on floppy disc handling in any training material or user guides provided. Always remember: (1) if a floppy becomes bent or crinkled it will not sit properly on the disc drive; (2) if magnetisation properties of the oxide film on which data is recorded are impaired, errors will occur; (3) pressure compacts the magnetic particles and alters the magnetic field or can dent the disc putting the surface just that bit too far from the read/write head. Since this is an area of significant abuse the major points are worth emphasising.

1. Floppies should be returned to their

jackets immediately after use. Discs should be kept away from ash-trays and other items that can cause contamination.

2. The exposed surface of a floppy should never be touched. Never press heavily when writing on a label attached to the cover, felt-tip pen should be used or better still the label written before sticking it on the floppy disc.

3. Only labels supplied by the floppy disc manufacturer should be used as these are designed to peel-off and be replaced as reference details change. New labels should definitely not be stuck over old ones as this will increase the thickness of the floppy.

4. Discs should be clearly labelled with correct information as to their reference and contents. Under no circumstances should correcting fluid be used on a label, as this will increase the thickness of the floppy and corruptions may be caused by flakes from the dried fluid.

5. Floppies should not be stored where there is regular magnetic or electrical interference or where the surface may get damp or exposed to strong sunlight. Extremes of temperature should be avoided: too high and the floppy crinkles and becomes unusable, too low and the magnetic film on which the data is stored loses some of its magnetisation.

6. Objects should not be rested on discs, particularly heavy ones. Paper clips or rubber bands should not be used on discs.

7. When mailing or transporting floppies a protective envelope or casing should be used – containers specially designed for this purpose are now available.

8. Discs should never be taken out of drives while being read from or written to and drives should not be switched on or off with the discs still present.

9. Inspect the discs as a matter of course for scratches and warping and take preventative action by copying everything onto a new disc before a permanent disc error or corruption occurs.

Finally, *treat floppy discs with respect*. They are

precision engineered and crucial to the operation of the system.

Guidelines and procedures

The following items should be decided upon and where appropriate considered for incorporation in guidance notes or clearly defined practices and procedures.

System Organisation

1. Allocation and naming of discs.
2. Document logging.
3. Minimum number of formatted discs to be held ready for use.
4. Establishing regular disc "tidy-up" sessions when originators are asked to check disc indexes to delete unwanted documents.
5. Record keeping of throughput and consumption of consumables.
6. Equipment maintenance practices.
7. Logging and dealing with peculiar and fault-type situations, tips and possible enhancements.
8. What to do on possible disc corruption.
9. Emergency procedures when the system goes down for a number of hours.

Document Matters

1. When passwords are to be used, where these are recorded and who is informed.
2. Recommendations on use of different typestyles.
3. Recommendations on the use of stationery.
4. Printed copies of standard formats or text, some of which may need to be set up or copied onto each new disc. It can also help in laying out complicated formats to have available a printed grid of characters at each position on an A4 page. All such records should be held in an easily accessible folder. Another useful listing to hold is of all the characters on each typestyle used (called a printwheel or thimble mapping).
5. When to take secure copies or when to remove a document to an archive store.
6. Details that an originator should provide in submitting a document for input to the system and use of a form if one has been designed.
7. Recommending the use of coloured pens by originators to mark-up drafts. This helps the operator to readily pick out the corrections needed.
8. Guidelines on tasks that can just as well be carried out on a typewriter rather than the word processing system.

Shared System or Bureau Operation

1. Required advance warning of bookings on the system and minimum/maximum time-slots.
2. Charging procedures – what is charged for, how often and what records need to be kept.
3. Nominating recognised users who can be left in charge of the system.
4. Responsibilities in relation to others using the system – who is responsible for discs, daisywheels, use of ribbons.

Appendix 3
Checklist for investing in word processing

We have devised a checklist for the complete exercise of investing in word processing equipment. It is based on major headings from the checklists to each chapter. The intention is that readers can quickly refer back to these for a list of more detailed points if need be, and from there to the text if necessary. This final checklist is in two major sections, "Planning and Preparation" and "Equipment Evaluation".

Planning and preparation

Organisational Issues (Chapter 3)

1. Consider the arrangement of word processing services within the organisation.

2. Decide on management responsibilities for a word processing function.

3. Get people committed.

4. Consider the personnel issues.

Costs (Chapter 12)
Work on the basis of total cost of ownership.

Training and Staff Selection (Chapter 11)

1. Arrange for early staff familiarisation.

2. Make arrangements for operator, supervisor and originator training.

3. In selecting staff to be trained or in appointing new staff look for recommended attributes.

Selecting Equipment (Chapter 3)

1. Analyse your situation profiling the workload and benefits sought.

2. Find out about existing facilities in the organisation.

3. Prepare a specification of requirements.

4. Select a representative workload sample.

5. Carry out desk research.

6. Attend exhibitions, collect literature, arrange demonstrations.

7. Prepare a short-list.

8. Contact or visit existing customers.

9. Examine suppliers contracts and start negotiating (Chapter 13).

Planning the Installation (Chapter 9)

1. Consider the location for the system and its environment.

2. Plan the lay-out.

3. Select suitable office furniture.

System Operation (Chapter 10)

1. Define responsibilities for a system supervisor and for operators.

2. Devise and document a system for the disc library.

3. Devise procedures for work scheduling, system use, security arrangements, and maintenance.

Equipment evaluation

These headings are intended as prompts to the areas to be looked at in evaluating equipment. The more detailed listings at the end of chapters in Part II may be used to prepare your own checklist of aspects that are particularly important to you.

Hardware Considerations (Chapter 4)
These cover visual display, keyboard, printer and storage.

Visual display:

- screen size and control information;
- colour & contrast;
- character design;
- the cursor;
- screen text movement;
- screen manoeuverability.

Keyboard:

- "detached" or not, operator preferences;

- ☐ function and control keys – dedicated, grammatical, cursor movement;
- ☐ repeat key facility;
- ☐ numeric pad.

Printer:

- ☐ daisywheel, Spinwriter, golf-ball, dot matrix and ink-jet, quality v. speed v. cost, spacing increments;
- ☐ tractor-feed and single-sheet feeder attachments.

Storage:

- ☐ internal memory capacity;
- ☐ floppy discs – size, capacity and demands on the drives;
- ☐ hard discs for greater capacity and speed of access.

Software Considerations (Chapter 5)

These cover basic considerations, formatting, text movement, printing and house-keeping.

Basic Considerations:

- ☐ software use of work disc space;
- ☐ disc drive availability;
- ☐ use of menus;
- ☐ functions and the keyboard – overall ease of use;
- ☐ prompts and messages – important to the operator;
- ☐ disc and document access – names or numbers, duplication checks;
- ☐ screen display – control characters, line endings, margin markers;
- ☐ scrolling – extent of screen movement;
- ☐ storage during editing – can affect performance;
- ☐ document security during editing – resilience to operator error;
- ☐ restricted access to discs and documents – password facilities;
- ☐ page or document-based – save command, separate pagination;

- ☐ insert and overwrite modes – cut-open, character push, reformatting, insert only mode.

Formatting:

- ☐ margin setting and indentation – flexibility;
- ☐ right-hand justification – quality;
- ☐ hyphenation – hyphen-help facility;
- ☐ reformatting – while editing or on command;
- ☐ decimal tabs facility;
- ☐ column work – column-walk, editing within columns;
- ☐ marking alterations for proof-correction facility;
- ☐ pagination – flexibility, effect on performance, headings and footings;
- ☐ typist aids – spaces after full-stops, variable spacing, centring facilities, required join, upper-lower case conversion, infill codes, cancel underline, line drawing.

Text movement: maximum block size, merge-printing facilities.

Printing: background, effect on performance, page specification, interrupt facilities, sharing.

House-keeping utilities.

Additional facilities (Chapter 6)

These may cover:

- ☐ search-and-replace;
- ☐ sort;
- ☐ spell;
- ☐ glossary;
- ☐ arithmetic;
- ☐ forms mode;
- ☐ storing keystrokes;
- ☐ availability of other applications packages;
- ☐ communication links;
- ☐ compatibility.

Support (Chapter 7)

1. Facilities.
2. Documentation available.
3. Installation, warranty & maintenance services.
4. Enhancements possible.
5. Supplier reputation.

Consumables and Other Equipment Issues (Chapter 8)

1. Ancillary equipment: tractor-feed, single-sheet feeder, acoustic hood.
2. Consumables: print elements, ribbons, floppy discs, and stationery.

Index

Where a number of references are given for a topic, the more significant ones are highlighted.